HAWAII

cooking with aloha

elvira monroe

irish margah

Published by
WIDE WORLD PUBLISHING/TETRA
P.O. Box 476
San Carlos, CA 94070

Thirteenth Printing October 2003

Printed in the United States of America

ISBN: 1-884550-25-8

Library of Congress Catalog Number: 87-051516

Mahalo to Theo who introduced me to the magic of the Islands, to Kate for her encouragement, and to Mia— newly under their spell—for her special contributions to this book.

—Elvira Monroe

To my mother, whose meals have always been as much a joy to the eye as they are a delight to the taste.

—Irish Margah

CONTENTS

Once back on the mainland although you may not be able to recreate three day poi in wooden tubs, an underground oven of white hot lava stones with steaming banana stocks, dishes prepared with limpet (opihi), banana flowers or breadfruit, the flavor of the islands can still be yours with steaming lau laus, Kalua pig, mai tais, fried rice, papayas, pineapple and the many other recipes in this book. We hope to help you recreate the mood and enjoyment you found on your trip to the islands.

Ono kau kau spiced with aloha!

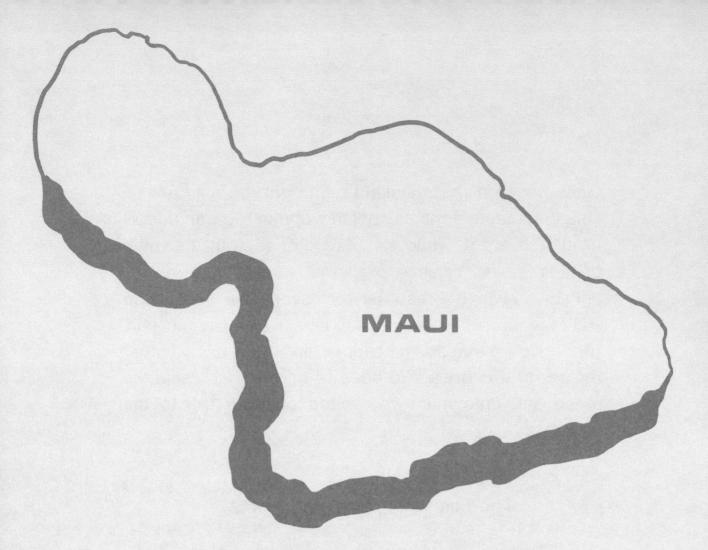

MAUI

THE VALLEY ISLAND

Flower—Roselani or lokelani

Color—Pink

"Maui no ka oi"—"Maui, the best of all"

Haleakala Crater   Lahaina

Seven Pools   Hana

Waianapanapa Cave   Iao Needle

DRINKS

ALCOHOLIC

SILVER SWORD FIZZ

1½ oz. gin
juice of ½ lemon
juice of ½ lime
1 oz cream
½ t powdered sugar
1 egg white

Shake vigorously with ice. Strain into glass over ice cubes. Fill with carbonated water. Stir. Makes 1 serving.

SINGAPORE SLING

9 oz gin
1½ oz brandy
2 T powdered sugar
juice of 2 lemons
6 maraschino cherries
6 pineapple slices
carbonated water

Mix gin, brandy, sugar, and lemon juice in cocktail shaker. Half fill highball glasses with cracked ice. Place a cherry and pineapple slice in each glass. Add liquor mixture. Finish filling glass with carbonated water. Makes 6 servings.

HAWAIIAN #1

1½ oz gin
¾ oz pineapple juice
dash of orange bitters
1 egg white

Combine gin, juice, bitters, and egg white in blender.
Whirl 15 seconds. Strain into cocktail glass. Makes 1
serving.

HAWAIIAN #2 OR
HULA-HULA COCKTAIL

2 oz gin
½ oz orange juice
½ oz curacao
crushed ice

Combine gin, juice and curacao in shaker. Shake well
with ice. Strain in cocktail glass. Makes 1 serving.

WAIKIKI BEACH COMBER

¾ oz gin
¾ oz triple sec
1 T pineapple juice, unsweetened
ice cubes

Combine gin, triple sec and juice. Shake with ice. Strain into glass.

PIÑA COLADA

3 oz light rum
3 T coconut milk
3 T pineapple, crushed
2 cups crushed ice

Place rum, coconut milk, pineapple, and ice in blender. Whirl until smooth at high speed. Garnish with pineapple. Serve with straw. *For the aloha touch, serve in coconut shell halves.*

FROZEN DAIQUIRI

1½ oz light rum
1½ oz lime juice
1 T triple sec
1 t sugar
crushed ice
maraschino cherry

Combine rum, lime juice, triple sec, sugar, and ice in blender. Blend at low speed briefly, then at high speed. Pour into champagne or cocktail glass. Add maraschino cherry.

FROZEN PINEAPPLE DAIQUIRI

1½ oz light rum
4 pineapple chunks
1 T lime juice
½ t sugar
1 cup crushed ice

Combine rum, pineappple, lime juice, sugar, and crushed ice in blender. Blend at low speed.

SUE AND DON WALLACE'S FRUIT DAIQUIRI

1 can frozen lemonade concentrate, pink
  use can as measure
1 can light rum
1 peach or papaya
ice cubes

Combine concentrate, rum, peach or papaya, and ice cubes in blender. Whirl 30 seconds. Serves 4.

For the aloha touch, serve in coconut shell halves.

HAWAIIAN CHAMPAGNE

½ t rum
½ t creme de banana liqueur
champagne, well chilled
banana slice

Combine rum and banana liqueur. Pour into champagne glass. Fill glass with champagne. Stir. Garnish with banana slice.

HARRY'S KANAKA HIGH

1½ oz bourbon whiskey
ice cubes
water

Pour whiskey over ice cubes. Add water to taste. Stir gently. Makes 1 serving.

HALEAKALA SUNRISE

2 oz light rum
2 oz pineapple juice, unsweetened
2 oz orange juice
¾ oz grenadine syrup
ice cubes

Combine rum, orange and pineapple juices, and ice cubes. Stir. Fill large glass with ice. Strain rum mixture into glass. Pour in grenadine slowly. Allow to settle. Just before serving, stir slightly. *The effect will be that of a sunrise at the Haleakala Crater on Maui.*

SCORPION

6 oz light rum
1 oz brandy
1 oz gin
6 oz lemon juice
6 oz orange juice
2 oz orgeat syrup or amaretto
ice cubes

Combine rum, brandy, gin, orange and lemon juices and orgeat syrup. Mix in blender with ice 30 seconds. Pour into bowl filled with cracked ice. *Float gardenia on top.* Serve with long straws. Serves 4. Or serve in champagne glasses. *Float gardenia in each glass.* Serves 4.

HONOLULU COCKTAIL #1

1½ oz gin
¼ t orange juice
¼ t pineapple juice
¼ t lemon juice
½ t powdered sugar

Combine gin, orange, pineapple and lemon juices in shaker. Shake. Strain into cocktail glass. Makes 1 serving.

HONOLULU COCKTAIL #2
OR HONOLULU LULU

1 oz gin
1 oz Benedictine
1 oz maraschino juice
crushed ice

Combine gin, Benedictine, and juice in shaker. Stir well with ice. Strain into cocktail glass. Makes 1 serving.

MAI TAI #1

2 oz light rum
1 oz triple sec
1 T orgeat syrup
1 T grenadine syrup
½ t powdered sugar
1 T lime juice
pineapple wedge
maraschino cherry
crushed ice

Combine rum, triple sec, orgeat and grenadine syrups, powdered sugar, and lime juice. Shake well with ice. Strain into glass 1/3 full with crushed ice. Serve with maraschino cherry speared to a wedge of pineapple. Serve with straw. Makes one serving.

For the aloha touch, float an orchid in the drink.

GIN ALOHA

1½ oz gin
1½ t triple sec
1 T pineapple juice, unsweetened
dash orange bitters
ice cubes

Combine gin, triple sec, pineapple juice, orange bitters, and ice. Shake. Pour into cocktail glass. Makes 1 serving.

MAI TAI #2

½ oz orange curacao or orgeat syrup
1 oz pineapple juice, unsweetened
½ oz lime juice
¼ oz orange triple sec or cointreau
1 oz light rum
1 oz dark rum
crushed ice
mint sprig
pineapple slice

Combine curacao or orgeat, pineapple and lime juices, triple sec, and rums. Mix well. Pour over crushed ice. Garnish with mint and pineapple or maraschino cherry speared to a wedge of pineapple. Makes 1 serving.
For the aloha touch, serve in a scooped out small pineapple or pineapple half.

CHI CHI

6 oz gin
8 oz pineapple juice, unsweetened
4 oz cream of coconut
2 oz heavy cream
¼ oz orange liqueur
2 cups crushed ice

Combine gin, pineapple juice, cream of coconut, cream, liqueur and crushed ice in blender. Whirl until smooth. Pour over crushed ice. Garnish with pineapple. Serve with straws. Makes 4 servings.

For the aloha touch, serve in coconut shell halves.

HONOLULU CUP

3 T rum
1 T lime juice
¼ cup pineapple juice, unsweetened
1½ t maraschino cherry juice
pineapple slice
mint sprig

Combine rum, lime, pineapple, and maraschino juices in a blender. Add cracked ice. Whirl 15 seconds. Fill a tall glass 2/3 full of crushed ice. Strain drink mixture into glass. Garnish with pineapple and mint. Makes 1 serving.

PLANTER'S PUNCH

2 oz light rum
1 t pineapple juice
juice of 1 lemon
juice of 1 lime
juice of 1 orange
ice
1 oz dark rum
orange and pineapple slice
maraschino cherry

Combine rum, pineapple, lemon lime and orange juices.
Pour into chilled or frosted glass. Add dark rum. Stir.
Garnish with slices of orange, pineapple, and maraschino
cherry skewered on long toothpick.

FISH HOUSE PUNCH

juice of 6 lemons
½ lb powdered sugar
½ pt brandy
¼ pt peach brandy
¼ pt rum
3 qts sparkling water, chilled

Place a large block of ice in a punch bowl. Add lemon
juice, sugar, brandies, rum, and sparkling water. Stir.
Makes 20 servings.

PINEAPPLE-ORANGE PUNCH

3 6 oz cans frozen pineapple juice concentrate
3 6 oz cans frozen orange juice concentrate
2 6 oz cans frozen lemonade concentrate
½ cup white corn syrup
1 bottle sherry
3 quarts water, chilled
2 quarts ginger ale

Combine pineapple, orange, and lemonade concentrates, corn syrup, and wine. Mix well. Refrigerate for several hours. Pour into punch bowl over block of ice or ice cubes. Add water and ginger ale. Stir until blended. Makes 60 servings.

CHAMPAGNE SHERBET PUNCH

2 bottles champagne, well chilled
1 bottle sauterne, well chilled
1 qt pineapple sherbet
1 cup pineapple, diced

Put sherbet in punch bowl. Pour over sauterne and champagne. Garnish with pineapple. Serves 12.

BANANA PUNCH

2 oz. vodka
1½ t apricot brandy
1 T lime juice
carbonated water
banana slices

Combine vodka, brandy and lime juice in a highball glass. Stir. Add carbonated water. Garnish with banana slices. Makes 1 serving.

TROPICAL ORANGE PUNCH

2 T orange spice tea, loose
12 cloves
¼ t ginger
1 quart boiling water
1 can frozen orange juice concentrate
1 quart apple juice, chilled
1 cup rum
1 quart sparkling water, chilled
orange slices

Combine tea, cloves, and ginger in a large teapot or jar. Pour in boiling water. Steep ½ hour. Strain. Chill. Pour into a punch bowl. Stir in orange juice concentrate, apple juice, and rum. When ready to serve, pour in sparkling water. Float orange slices on top. Makes 20 servings.

NON-ALCOHOLIC

POI COCKTAIL

1 cup milk
2 T mixed poi
2 to 3 t sugar
¼ t vanilla
ice cubes
dash of nutmeg

Place milk, poi, sugar, vanilla, and ice in blender. Blend thoroughly. Serve topped with nutmeg. Makes 2 servings.

ISLAND COOLER

½ cup lemon juice
1 cup orange juice
¼ cup pineapple juice, unsweetened
grated lemon rind
1 bottle ginger ale
crushed ice or ice cubes
mint sprig

Combine lemon, orange, and pineapple juices. Half fill tall glasses with ice. Pour in juice mixture. Sprinkle with lemon rind. Fill with ginger ale. Stir. Garnish with mint. Serves 4.

GRAPEFRUIT—PINEAPPLE COOLER

½ cup grapefruit juice, chilled
2 cups pineapple juice, unsweetened, chilled
1 cup ginger ale, chilled

Combine grapefruit and pineapple juice. When ready to serve, add ginger ale. Pour over cracked ice. Serves 4.

CHILLED COCONUT DRINK

Chill coconut several hours or overnight. Punch out eyes. Insert straws. Sip, and remember the blue sky and sea and the palms swaying in the tradewinds. When finished, crack coconut and eat coconut meat.

QUICK FRUIT PUNCH

1 cup tropical fruit punch (canned)
2¼ cups pineapple juice, unsweetened
2½ cups guava or papaya nectar
½ lemon juice
1 T mint, finely chopped

Combine tropical punch and pineapple, guava, and lemon juices. Stir in mint. Pour over crushed ice. Serves 8.

PUNCH SERVED AT WAIOLI TEA ROOM, HONOLULU

5 cups guava juice, chilled
5 cups passion fruit juice, chilled
5 cups pineapple juice, chilled
1 cup lemon juice
4 cups sugar

Combine guava, passion fruit, pineapple, and lemon juices. Add sugar. Stir until sugar is dissolved. Pour over ice block or ice cubes. Garnish with orange slices.

BASIC HONOLULU PUNCH

2 parts pineapple juice, unsweetened
1 part ginger ale, chilled
    maraschino cherry juice or grenadine syrup

Combine pineapple juice and ginger ale according to quantity desired. Tint with maraschino juice or grenadine. Pour over crushed ice.

ALOHA FRUIT PUNCH

¾ cup water
2 t ginger root, chopped
2 cups guava juice
1½ T lemon juice
1½ cups pineapple, finely chopped
1 cup sugar

Add ¼ cup water to ginger root. Boil 3 minutes. Strain. Add the liquid to the guava, lemon, and pineapple juices. Make a syrup of sugar and remaining water. Cool. Combine with juices and pineapple. Chill thoroughly. Serves 8.

SHERBET PUNCH

1 quart boiling water

8 tea bags, or enough loose tea to make 1 quart

2 cups orange juice

1 cup lemon juice

1 quart pineapple juice

2 cups apricot nectar

2 cups sugar

1 quart ginger ale

1 quart raspberry, lime, or pineapple sherbet

Prepare 1 quart of tea. Chill. Combine with orange, lemon, and pineapple juices and apricot nectar. Add sugar. Stir until sugar is dissolved. When ready to serve, add ginger ale. Pour over block of ice or ice cubes in punch bowl. Spoon in sherbet. Makes 24 servings.

BANANA SHAKE

2 bananas, sliced
4 cups milk
1 pint vanilla ice cream, softened
½ t vanilla

Put bananas in blender. Add milk and vanilla. Blend 30 seconds. Add ice cream. Blend 1 minute. Makes 4 servings.

MOCHA SHAKE

2 cups strong coffee, chilled
¾ cup chocolate milk
1½ cups coffee ice cream

Combine coffee, chocolate milk, and ice cream in blender. Beat until smooth. Makes 4 servings.

PAPAYA SHAKE

2 cups papaya pulp
2/3 cup sugar
1/4 cup lemon juice
3 cups milk
1 t nutmeg
6 to 8 ice cubes

Combine papaya and sugar in blender. Add lemon juice. Blend thoroughly. Add milk. Whirl for 15 seconds. Add ice cubes. Whirl 20 seconds longer. Sprinkle with nutmeg.

PAPAYA-BANANA SMOOTHIE

1 cup papaya pulp
1/2 cup banana, sliced
1 cup guava juice
2/3 cup pineapple juice, unsweetened
2 T lemon juice
1/3 cup sugar
  crushed ice

Combine papaya, banana, guava, pineapple and lemon juices, and sugar in blender. Blend 2 minutes until thoroughly mixed. Pour in tall glass over crushed ice.

PAPAYA–PINEAPPLE SMOOTHIE

1 papaya
1 cup pineapple juice, unsweetened
water
honey

Cut papaya in chunks. Whirl in blender with pineapple juice. Add enough water to make it a good drinking consistency. Sweeten to taste with honey. Makes 2 servings.

CREAMY BANANA SMOOTHIE

1 banana, cut up
½ cup milk
1 T honey
⅛ t vanilla
ice cubes

Combine banana, milk, honey, vanilla, and ice in blender. Blend until smooth. Makes 2 servings.

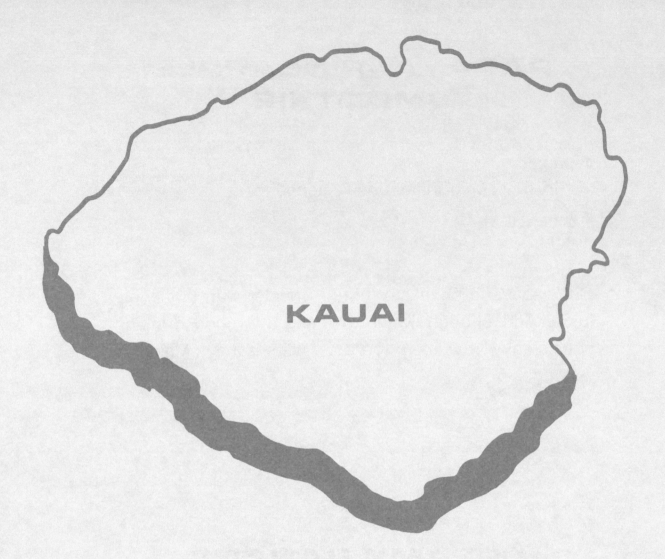

KAUAI

THE GARDEN ISLAND

Flower—Mokihana Berry

Color—Purple

Waimea Canyon   Fern Grotto

Hanalei—setting for movie "South Pacific"

Spouting Horn   Na Pali Coast

PUPUS

'ONO 'ONO SPARERIBS

4 to 5 lbs lean spareribs
water
2 t salt
Tangy Barbeque Glaze

Ask butcher to crack bones to make 3" to 4" lengths. Place ribs in large saucepan. Add water to cover. Add salt. Bring to boil. Lower heat. Cover. Simmer 30 minutes or until ribs are almost tender.

Drain ribs well. Cut into 1 rib sections. Place in shallow glass dish. Pour glaze over. Let ribs marinate for several hours or overnight in refrigerator.

Drain ribs. Reserve glaze. Place ribs on grill. Grill 20 to 30 minutes. Turn often and brush generously with glaze until ribs are browned and evenly glazed.

RUMAKI

10 water chestnuts, halved
5 chicken livers, quartered
10 slices bacon, cut in half
soy sauce and ginger marinade

Wrap water chestnut half and piece of chicken liver in bacon slice. Pierce with toothpick. Refrigerate in marinade for 2 hours. Broil, over charcoal or in broiler, basting and turning, until bacon is crisp.

WON TON

¼ lb ground pork
1 T minced shrimp
1 t ginger juice *from fresh ginger*
½ t salt
1 T soy sauce
1 T wine
1 T water chestnuts, chopped or celery, chopped
Won Ton Pi or Won Ton Skin*

Mix pork, shrimp, ginger juice, salt, soy sauce, wine, and celery or water chestnuts.

Place ½ t of filling in center of wrapping. Fold the won ton skin as follows.

Deep fry. Serve hot. Dip in sweet-sour sauce.

Buy in a Chinese grocery store or restaurant, if it is not available at your grocery or supermarket.

TERIYAKI RIBS

4 lbs meaty pork spareribs
Teriyaki Marinade

Ask butcher to saw ribs in half across bones. Cut into 2 rib portions. Place in shallow baking dish. Pour marinade over ribs. Cover. refrigerate 6 to 8 hours, or overnight. Remove ribs. Drain, reserving marinade. Place on grill bone side down. Grill 25 minutes over low coals. Turn. Grill 15 to 20 minutes. Brush with marinade.

31

BUTTERFLIED COCONUT SHRIMP

1 lb large shrimp
oil
¼ cup flour
½ t salt
1 egg
2 T cream of coconut
¾ cup coconut, flaked
1/3 cup packaged bread crumbs
Chinese Mustard Sauce

Shell and devein shrimp, leaving tails on. Slit shrimp with sharp knife along curved side, cutting almost through. Pour oil 2" deep into saucepan. Heat to 350°. While oil is heating, combine flour, salt, and dry mustard in a small bowl, beat egg and cream of coconut. In a third bowl combine coconut and bread crumbs.

Dip shrimp in flour mixture, then in egg mixture, then in crumb mixture, coating well. Refrigerate until ready to cook.

When oil is hot, fry shrimps a few at a time, turning once, for 2 minutes or until golden. Remove with slotted spoon. Drain on paper toweling. Serve hot. Serve with *Chinese Mustard Sauce*.

SHRIMP KABOBS

18 large shrimps or prawns
1 can water chestnuts
1 cup pineapple, cut in cubes
any *Soy Sauce Marinade*

Place shrimps in a bowl. Cover with marinade. Refrigerate 1 hour. Drain. Alternate shrimp, water chestnuts, and pineapple on long bamboo skewers. Cook over hibachi or in oven for 5 minutes on each side.

SEAFOOD ON A SKEWER

Assorted cubes of salmon, cod, any white fish, scallops, shrimp, or lobster
mushrooms
cherry tomatoes
red and green peppers
onions·
pineapple chunks
marinade of your choice

Marinate seafood. Oil skewers. Alternate seafoods, vegetable and onions on skewers according to taste. Cook over hibachi or barbeque until done.

BEEF TERIYAKI

1½ lbs top round steak, cut 1 inch thick.

Teriyaki marinade

Pierce steak deeply all over with a fork. Place in shallow, non-metal dish or bowl.

Pour about 1/3 over steak. Cover. Refrigerate several hours or overnight. Turn steak once or twice.

Cut meat into long thin slices about 1/8″ thick. Thread accordion-style on 8″ bamboo skewers. Brush with marinade. Broil, 2 to 3 inches from heat, one minute. Turn and broil 1 minute longer. Serve with reserved marinade.

MEAT BALLS AND
WATER CHESTNUTS

½ lb lean ground beef

½ lb bulk sausage or ground pork

2 cups bread cubes

½ cup milk

½ t onion powder

1 t garlic salt

1 T soy sauce

½ t tabasco

1 can water chestnuts, drained & chopped

¼ cup oil

Soak bread cubes in milk. Squeeze out as much milk as possible. Add to beef and pork. Add onion powder, garlic salt, soy sauce, and tabasco. Shape into about 48 small balls. Brown in oil. Serve hot with toothpicks.

COCONUT (NI'U) CHIPS

Remove coconut meat from coconut. Keep pieces as large as possible. Do not remove brown peel. Slice very thin. Spread on cookie sheet. Bake at 200° for 2 hours. Reduce heat to 150°. Bake for 2 additional hours. Turn several times while baking. Remove from oven. Cool. Store in air tight container.

PORK BALLS

1 lb ground pork
1 can water chestnuts, drained and finely chopped
½ cup green onions, finely chopped
1 t fresh or crystallized ginger, finely chopped
¾ t salt
1 T soy sauce
1 egg, lightly beaten
½ cup packaged bread crumbs
cornstarch
3 T oil
Sweet and Sour Sauce

Combine pork, water chestnuts, green onions, ginger, salt, soy sauce, and egg in large bowl. Mix well with hands. Add bread crumbs. Mix until combined. Chill 1 hour. Shape into 36 balls. Roll in cornstarch to coat lightly. Shake off excess.

Heat oil until sizzling in a large skillet. Add meatballs and brown on all sides. Remove to a roasting pan. Cover loosely with foil.

Bake at 350° for 20 minutes. Place in a serving dish. Stir in enough *Sweet and Sour Sauce* to coat.

SESAME CHICKEN WINGS

18 chicken wings
2 T sesame seeds
3/4 cup packaged bread crumbs
1 t paprika
1/2 t salt
1/3 cup heavy cream
1/2 cup butter, melted
Polynesian glaze

Shake sesame seeds in small skillet over low heat until golden. Cut each chicken wing into tow sections, making a "drum stick" and outer wing portion. Combine sesame seeds, bread crumbs, paprika and salt. Dip chicken pieces in cream, coating completely. Roll in crumb mixture. Refrigerate 1 hour. Place butter in 13" x 9" x 2" baking dish. Melt in oven while oven preheats to 375°. Remove from oven. Turn chicken in butter, coating completely. Bake at 375° for 40 minutes.
Serve with Polynesian Glaze

DEVILED EGGS

For variety add chopped black olives, horseradish, minced dill pickles, or jalapeno peppers to chopped hard cooked eggs.

CHICKEN WINGS IN SOY SAUCE

18 chicken wings

Soy sauce marinade or soy sauce and ginger marinade

Cut wings at middle joint, making a "drum stick" and outer wing portion.* Bring marinade to a simmer. Add chicken. Simmer for 25 minutes. Remove from marinade. Broil 3 minutes on each side. Serve hot or cold.

Some stores sell chicken wings already cut and pack-aged in this way.

CURRIED PEANUTS

2 cups unsalted roasted peanuts
2 t curry powder

Spread peanuts on cookie sheet or roasting pan. Sprinkle with curry powder.
Warm in 300° oven.

ROASTED MACADAMIA NUTS

Roasting macadamia nuts in a 250° oven for a few minutes enhances the flavor. Serve hot.

RAW FISH

Use any white fish. Strip fish, then dice it. Dip in soya sauce. *Wash down with beer.*

POISON CREUX

raw white fish, diced
½ cup coconut milk
½ cup lime juice

Marinate fish in coconut milk and lime juice for at least 1 hour.

MACADAMIA CHEDDAR CHEESE BALLS

1 8 oz pkg cream cheese, softened
¼ cup butter, softened
2½ cups extra sharp cheddar cheese, shredded
¼ cup chutney, finely chopped
1 cup macadamia nuts, chopped
chopped parsley

Beat cream cheese and butter in large bowl with electric mixer until smooth. Beat in cheddar cheese. Stir in chutney. Chill overnight.

Shape into balls of 1 t each. Roll in nuts and parsley. Refrigerate until ready to serve.

MUSHROOMS STUFFED WITH CRAB

3 dozen large fresh mushrooms
8 oz crab meat
1 T parsley, finely minced
1 T pimiento, chopped
¼ t dry mustard
½ cup mayonnaise

Remove stems from mushrooms. Combine crab, parsley, and pimiento. Blend mustard into mayonnaise. Toss into crab mixture. Fill each mushroom crown with about 2 T crab mixture. Bake at 375° for 8 to 10 minutes.

CHUTNEY CREAM CHEESE SPREAD

1 8 oz pkg. cream cheese
¼ cup chutney
¼ cup half and half

Blend cream cheese, chutney, and half and half. Add additional half and half, as necessary, to moisten to spreading consistency. Spread on crackers.

PINEAPPLE WITH RUM

2 cups pineapple, cubed
2 cups sugar
1 cup water
3 oz rum
2 T lemon or lime juice
1 t amaretto

In a saucepan, combine sugar and water. Stir over low heat until sugar dissolves. Cool. Add rum, lemon or lime juice, and amaretto. Stir well. Dip pineapple in syrup.

For the aloha touch, serve syrup in partially scooped out pineapple shell.

CREAM CHEESE CRISPS

1 3 oz pkg cream cheese, softened
1 cup flour
¾ t salt
¼ cup shortening
¼ cup parsley, finely chopped
2 T water

Sift flour and salt together. Blend in shortening and cream cheese. Add parsley and water. Mix until dough is dry and crumbly. Put on lightly floured bread board. Press dough together. Roll out to ⅛" thickness. Using a biscuit cutter, cut into 2" circles. Place on ungreased cookie sheet. Bake at 425° for 10 minutes—until lightly browned. Makes 3 dozen.

CURRY DIP

2 8 oz cream cheese, softened

¼ cup sherry

1 t curry powder

¾ cup sour cream

Beat cream cheese, sherry and curry until smooth Blend in sour cream.

BACON & CURRY DIP

1 8 oz pkg cream cheese, softened

½ cup mayonnaise or plain yogurt

6 strips bacon, fried crisp & crumbled

  or

1 small can deviled ham

curry powder to taste

chopped parsley

Combine cream cheese, mayonnaise, bacon and curry. Blend well. Press in a round bowl. Refrigerate for ½ hour. Turn out on center of a serving dish. Garnish with chopped parsley. Serve with assorted raw vegetables.

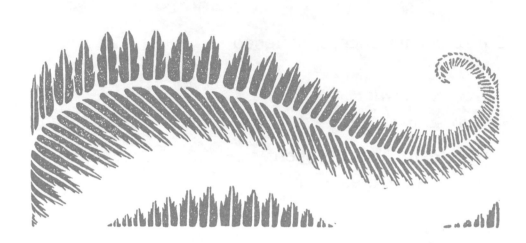

AVOCADO DIP

2 avocados, mashed
¼ cup mayonaise
2 T lemon juice
1 t chili powder
1 garlic clove, mashed
Maui potato chips

Add mayonaise, lemon juice, chili powder, and garlic to avocados. Mix well. Cover. Let stand 1 hour. *Serve with Maui potato chips*.

CHUTNEY CREAM CHEESE DIP WITH SHERRY

2 8 oz pkg cream cheese, softened
¼ cup dry sherry
½ t curry powder
½ c chutney
2 T green onion, chopped
¾ cup sour cream

Beat cream cheese, sherry and curry powder until smooth. Stir in chutney and green onions. Mix well. Add sour cream. Blend.

LANAI

THE PINEAPPLE ISLAND

Flower—Kaunaoa

Color—Orange

Garden of the Gods

Shipwreck Beach   Kaunolu Village

MAIN DISHES

LANAI SIRLOIN STEAK

1 sirloin steak, 1½" to 2" thick.
Teriyaki marinade

Score fat edges of meat. Place in shallow non-metal dish. Pour marinade over meat. Cover. Marinate at room temperature for 2 to 3 hours, or 6 hours refrigerated. Turn often. Remove from marinade. Drain well. Grill 5" to 6" from grayed coals, 20 minutes on each side for rare. Brush often with marinade.

BEEF TERIYAKI

Teriyaki marinade #1 or #2

Slice meat thinly across the grain. Soak in marinade 30 minutes. Drain. Broil 5 to 10 minutes, or until brown. Turn, and brown on other side. Makes 6 servings.

KUN KOKI

Korean Broiled Steak

1½ lbs. flank steak
Korean Marinade

Trim, pound and score steak. Cut into 3" x 4" pieces. Spread marinade on steak. Marinate for 1 hour. Broil 4 minutes. Turn. Broil 3 minutes. Serves 6.

BEEF KABOBS

2½ lbs beef sirloin steak, cut in 1½" pieces
3 green peppers, cut in 1" squares
5 tomatoes, quartered
Soy Sauce Marinade

Place meat in a baking dish. Pour on marinade. Cover. Refrigerate several hours or overnight. Drain, saving marinade. Alternate beef, pepper, and tomatoes on skewers. Grill over medium-hot coals 15 minutes or additional time according to taste. Baste occasionally with marinade. Makes 8 servings.

PICKLED PORTUGUESE ROAST

3 to 4 lb roast
2 cloves garlic, crushed
1 T salt
2 T vinegar
3 dried red peppers, crushed and marinated in vinegar
½ cup water

Mix garlic, salt, vinegar, and water. Marinate meat in mixture for ½ hour. Roast meat in marinade at 325°. Allow 30 minutes per pound. Baste frequently. Serve with pickled white or *Maui* onions.

HAWAIIAN SHORTRIBS

6 lbs beef shortribs, cut into 2" lengths
½ cup flour
2 cups onions, sliced
1 cup catsup
3 T vinegar
2 T soy sauce
2 T Worcestershire Sauce
½ cup sugar
1 cup water

Roll shortribs in flour. Arrange in large casserole or roaster. Cover with sliced onions. Combine catsup, vinegar, soy sauce, Worcestershire Sauce, sugar, and water. Mix well. Pour over ribs. Cover. Bake at 350° for 2 to 2½ hours. serves 6.

KOREAN BARBEQUED SHORT RIBS

8 lbs beef short ribs, cut into 1½ in pieces
Korean Marinade

Cut across meat side of each short rib piece through to the bone in checkerboard design. Make slashes about ⅛ apart on remaining meat on sides of bone. Soak ribs in marinade ½ hour. Broil over hot charcoal fire.

LINGUISA FILLING FOR OMELETTE

2 lbs boneless pork
2½ cups water
1 t vinegar
4 cloves garlic, mashed
⅛ t cumin
1 t salt
¼ t pepper
chili peppers or tabasco to taste

Remove fat from pork. Chop pork into as small pieces as possible. Place in bowl. Add water, vinegar, garlic, cinnamon, cumin and salt and pepper. Mix well. Cover. Refrigerate 2 days. Stir several times. Add peppers or tabasco to taste. Drain off liquid. Squeeze out moisture. Fry in skillet 6 to 8 minutes.

ORANGE AND CHUTNEY HAM

8 lb ham
1 can frozen orange juice concentrate
½ cup brown sugar,packed
4 T chutney
2 T sherry
pineapple slices

Bake ham at 325° for 2 hours. Remove rind. Combine orange concentrate,sugar,chutney and sherry. Brush again. Return to oven for 1 hour. Baste several times with orange-chuntney mixture. Makes 8 servings.

ADOBO FILIPINO

3 lbs pork chops, 1" thick
2 cloves garlic,minced
4 bay leaves
¾ cup vinegar
¾ cup water
1½ t salt
dash of pepper
3 bunches spinach,cooked

Place pork,garlic,bay leaves,vinegar,water,and salt and pepper in a skillet. Soak 5 minutes. Cover. Bring to boil quickly. Lower heat. Simmer until almost dry. Remove chops. Toss spinach in skillet. Sprinkle with vinegar. Serves 6.

SPIT ROASTED PORK LOIN

1 6 to 7 lb loin of pork
2 t salt
Polynesian Glaze or *Tangy Barbecue Glaze*

Rub pork with salt and place on spit. Set spit in position over hot coals. Start rotisserie. Grill 1½ hours. Allow 30 to 35 minutes per pound. Brush part of glaze over pork. Continue grilling and brushing often with more glaze, for 1 hour or until meat is tender and richly glazed. Remove to cutting board. Take out spit. Carve into slices. Serve with remaining glaze as a sauce.

ROAST LOIN OF PORK

3½ lb loin of pork
2 T crystallized ginger, finely chopped
¼ cup soy sauce
watercress

Preheat oven to 325°. Makes several small small slits at intervals in pork. Insert 1 T of the chopped ginger in the slits. Combine remaining ginger and soy sauce. Place pork fat side up, in roasting pan. Do not use a rack. Brush pork with part of soy mixture. Cook 1 hour and 45 minutes. Brush with soy mixture several times during roasting. Remove from oven. Wait 20 minutes. Carve.

Put pork on wooden board and garnish with watercress. Arrange Bananas Baked in Orange Juice around roast. Serves 6.

CHINESE ROAST PORK

2½ lbs boneless lean pork
marinade of your choice

Cut pork in strips 1″ wide. Marinate overnight in marinade of your choice. Place on rack in baking pan. Roast at 350° for 1 hour, or until done. Baste every 15 minutes with marinade. Remove from oven. Cool. Cut in very thin diagonal slices. Serve with *Chinese mustard* and catsup.

SWEET and SOUR PORK CHOPS

4 pork chops
½ cup celery,chopped
¼green pepper,chopped
1 tomato, cubed
1 cup pineapple, cubed
sweet and sour sauce

Cook pork chops until well done. Saute celery and pepper until tender,but still somewhat crisp. Add tomato and pineapple. Cook 1 min. Place pork chops on platter. Cover with pineapple-vegetable mixture. Pour sauce over ingredients. Serve with steamed rice. Serves 4.

KALUA PIG

6 lb boneless pork butt
rock salt
ti or banana leaves
½ bottle liquid smoke
aluminum foil, heavy duty

Make deep slashes in pork. Rub rock salt into cuts. Spread ti or banana leaves on large sheet of aluminum foil. Place pork on leaves. Pour liquid smoke over pork. Wrap leaves around pork and tie together. Fold foil tightly around pork. Refrigerate overnight. Cook at 500^0 for 1 hour. Lower heat to 400^0. Cook 4 hours.

GINGER SPARERIBS WITH PINEAPPLE

4 lbs pork spareribs

1 clove garlic,minced

¼ cup soy sauce

¼ cup brown sugar

1 T ginger, freshly grated

1 onion sliced

1 green pepper, sliced

2 T oil

1 T cornstarch

2 T vinegar

1 can pineapple chunks and syrup

Roast ribs uncovered at 425° for 30 minutes.Drain off fat. Reduce heat to 325°. Combine garlic,soy,sugar, and ginger.Pour over ribs. Sauté onions and green pepper until tender.In a sauce pan, mix cornstarch,vinegar,and pineapple syrup. Cook for 1 minute, stirring constantly, until thick and transparent. Add pineapple. Pour over ribs. Bake uncovered at 325° 1 hour. Turn and baste every 15 minutes. Serves 4.

SWEET AND SOUR PORK

1 lb pork loin
2 T sherry
2 T soy sauce
3 T cornstarch
oil
Sweet and Sour Sauce

Cut pork into ½″ cubes. Combine pork, sherry, soy sauce, and cornstarch. Fry in oil until done.

Pour Sweet and Sour Sauce over pork.

Serve with steamed rice.

PANSIT FILIPINO

1 pkg noodles
1 T oil
1 clove garlic,crushed
1 onion sliced
1 lb pork,cubed
½ lb fresh shrimp
3 tomatoes, sliced
roasted peanuts,ground
fried eggs,cut in thin strips
lemon slices
finely chopped onions

Cook noodles. Drain. Heat oil in a skillet. Add garlic. Cook for a few minutes. Remove garlic. Add onion. Cook until soft. Add pork. Cook until meat is tender. Add shrimp when pork is half cooked. Add tomatoes. Heat thoroughly.

When ready to serve, place noodles in center of platter. Arrange meat,shrimp and tomato mixture around noodles. Garnish with peanuts,eggs,lemon,and onion. Makes 6 servings.

LAU LAUS

1 lb luau (taro leaves) or fresh spinach
1¼ lbs pork cut in 6 pieces
¾ lbs salmon or butter fish, cut in 6 pieces
1 T rock salt
12 ti leaves or aluminum foil
1 cup water
6 bananas
6 sweet potatoes or yams

Wash two taro leaves thoroughly. Remove stem and fibrous part of veins by pulling gently with the tip of a knife from the stem out to the edge of the leaves. Place pork in bowl. Add salt. Work together. Arrange 5 leaves, the largest on the bottom. Place pork with fat side up. Placefish on top of pork. Fold leaves over pork and fish to form a bundle (*puolo*). Prepare each ti leaf by cutting partially through the stiff rib and stripping it off. Place lau lau of the end of a ti leaf and wrap tightly. Wrap another ti leaf around in the opposite direction, thereby forming a flat package. Tie with string, or fibrous part of ti leaves. Place in a steamer. As soon as water is boiling,turn heat to low. Steam laulaus 5 to 6 hours. Add unpeeled sweet potatoes and bananas in their skins for the last hour. Makes 6 servings.

Remove string before serving.

MANDARIN CHICKEN WITH RICE

2½ lbs chicken

1 t salt

¼ t pepper

1 cup onions, chopped

1 clove garlic, crushed

1 T butter

¼ cup catsup

1/3 cup orange marmalade

2 T soy sauce

1 cup chicken stock

2 t dry mustard

1 green pepper, cut in strips

4 cups hot cooked rice

Season chicken with salt and pepper. Bake 30 minutes at 350°. Sauté onions and garlic in butter until soft. Add catsup, marmalade, soy sauce, chicken stock, and mustard. Simmer 15 minutes. Spoon over chicken. Bake 20 minutes. Stir in green pepper. Cook 5 minutes. Serve over steamed rice. Serves 6.

CHICKEN WITH SWEET POTATOES AND BANANAS

4 lb roasting chicken, cut into pieces

2 T oil

½ cup onion, chopped

1 clove garlic, crushed

2 T flour

1 t salt

¼ t pepper

1 bay leaf

1 cup chicken stock or 1 chicken bouillon cube, dissolved in 1 cup boiling water

1 8 oz can tomatoes, drained

2 large sweet potatoes, peeled and cut in 1½" slices

4 bananas, peeled and halved

2 T oil

Sauté chicken in skillet in oil until well browned. Remove from skillet. Pour off drippings. Sauté onion and garlic about 3 minutes, or until soft. Stir in flour, salt and pepper. Add bay leaf, chicken stock, and tomatoes. Mix well. Add ¾ cup water. Return chicken to skillet. Add sweet potatoes. Cover. Simmer 45 minutes. In another skillet, sauté bananas in oil until golden. When ready to serve, place chicken and potatoes on platter and surround with bananas. Serves 8.

CHICKEN & ALMOND

2 T oil

½ lb chicken breast, uncooked

1 cup bamboo shoots, cut up

1 cup celery, diced

½ cup Chinese chard, sliced

½ cup water chestnuts, diced

¼ cup blanched almonds, slivered

2 T soy sauce

1½ cups chicken stock, hot

2 T cornstarch

3 T cold water

1 cup rice, steamed

Sauté chicken in oil. Add bamboo shoots, celery, chard, water chestnuts, almonds, soy sauce, and chicken broth. Mix well. cover. Simmer 5 to 10 minutes. Combine cornstarch and water until smooth. Add to chicken mixture. Stir well. Serve over rice. Serves 2.

CHICKEN 'ONO NUI

3 T oil

6 T flour

3 cups milk

2 cups cooked chicken, diced

½ t salt

1 T pimiento, sliced

1 cup pineapple, diced

3 coconuts

Trim rough fiber from coconut shells. Saw in half cross-wise. Combine oil, flour and milk in a saucepan over low heat. Stir until you have a smooth white sauce. Add chicken, salt, pimiento, and pineapple. Fill coconut halves with chicken-pineapple mixture. Place in shallow baking pan. Bake at 350° for 1 hour. Coconut meat becomes firm and cannot be eaten. Serves 6.

Variation: Substitute tuna or turkey for chicken.

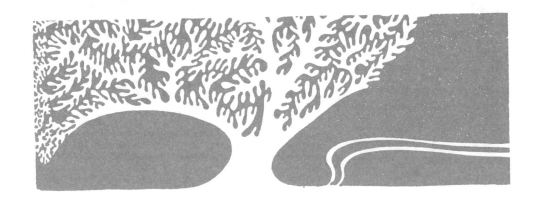

CHICKEN SUKIYAKI

3 lbs chicken, uncooked
3 T oil
1 onion, sliced
1 can bamboo shoots, sliced
½ cup sugar
¾ cup soy sauce
¾ cup hot water and mushroom liquid
1 can mushrooms
1 lb bean sprouts
5 green onions, sliced
1 tofu, cubed

Bone chicken. Fry in hot oil. Add onion and bamboo shoots. Add 3 T sugar, ¼ cup soy and ½ cup water-mushroom liquid. Boil 5 minutes. Add mushrooms, sprouts, and onions. Continue cooking. Stir in remaining sugar, soy and liquid a little at a time. Add tofu. Cook 10 to 15 minutes. Serves 6.

QUICK HAWAIIAN CHICKEN

1 green pepper, cut in strips

2 cloves garlic, minced

2 T oil

2 cans condensed cream of chicken soup, undiluted

2 cups pineapple chunks, with syrup

2 cups cooked chicken, diced

2 T soy sauce

3 cups cooked rice

½ cup slivered almonds or chopped macadamia nuts

Saute´ pepper and garlic in oil until pepper is soft. Blend in soup and pineapple syrup. Gently blend in chicken, pineapple and soy sauce. Heat thoroughly. Serve over rice. Garnish with nuts. Serves 6.

HULI HULI CHICKEN
(Turn and Turn Chicken)

3 fryers, quartered
¼ cup catsup
¼ cup soy sauce
½ cup chicken stock
3 T frozen pineapple concentrate
1 T ginger freshly chopped
2 T Worcestershire Sauce

Mix catsup, soy sauce, wine or chicken stock, pineapple concentrate, ginger, and Worcestershire sauce. Brush part over chicken. Grill, 5" to 6" from grayed coals. Turn often and baste often with sauce. Cook about 40 minutes or until chicken is browned and well done. Makes 12 servings.

CURRY WITH PINEAPPLE

3 cups milk
2 cups coconut
3 cloves garlic, minced
1 T ginger root, chopped
2 apples, cored and diced
2 onions, chopped
2 T curry powder
½ cup butter, softened
½ cup flour
½ t salt
½ cup cream
3 cups cooked chicken
1 cup pineapple, diced

Combine milk and coconut. Simmer. Add garlic, ginger, apples, and onions. Blend curry powder and 2 T butter. Add to coconut mixture. Cook at low heat for 3 hours. Stir occasionally. Remove from heat. Cool several hours, or overnight. Strain. Heat thoroughly over low heat. Blend flour with remaining butter. Add to mixture. Stir until mixture thickens. Stir in salt and cream. Add chicken and pineapple. Cook over low heat ½ hour.

For the aloha touch, serve curry in a scooped-out pineapple shell. Makes 6 servings. Serve with steamed rice.

Serve crisp chopped bacon, chutney, pickles, shredded coconut, chopped nuts, raisins, chopped hard cooked eggs, and dried apricots* as condiments.

*soak apricots in water. Drain. Chop finely.

CURRY IN A HURRY

1 can cream of mushroom soup, undiluted
1 T curry powder, or more according to taste
1 cup cooked chicken or shrimp
1 cup sour cream

Heat soup. Stir in curry. Add chicken of shrimp. Heat. Just before serving, add sour cream. Heat thoroughly. Serve over steamed rice.

SHRIMP CURRY

1 cup shrimp
2 T butter, melted
3 T curry powder
¼ cup onions, finely chopped
½ cup celery, finely chopped
½ cup bell pepper, finely chopped
1 cup white wine
1 cup papaya nectar
2 T chutney
¼ t nutmeg

Sauté butter and curry powder 1 minute. Add onions. Cook until soft. Add celery and pepper. Sauté until soft. Add wine, papaya nectar, chutney and nutmeg. Simmer 20 minutes until mixture thickens. Add cornstarch if necessary.

Add shrimp. Simmer 4 to 5 minutes. Serves 4.

CHICKEN AND SHRIMP CURRY

1 fryer, quartered

3 cups water

¼ cup butter

1 onion, diced

¼ cup flour

2 T curry powder, or more to taste

½ t salt

¼ t pepper

¼ t ground ginger

1½ cup coconut milk

⅛ cup lime juice

½ lb. shrimp, cooked, peeled, and deveined

1 cup pineapple chunks

Cook chicken. Save 3 cups chicken stock. Remove chicken meat from bones. Cut into bite-size pieces. Sauté onion in butter in large casserole or Dutch oven until tender. Remove from heat. Stir in flour, curry, salt, pepper, and ginger. Gradually stir in chicken stock. Stir in coconut milk.

Cook over low heat, stirring constantly, until mixture thickens and bubbles 2 minutes. Add lime juice, chicken, shrimp, and pineapple. Heat thoroughly. Serve with chutney, green onions, peanuts, raisins, kumquats, shredded coconut as condiments.

For the aloha touch, serve curry in hollowed-out pine-apple shells, cut lengthwise.

MAHI MAHI BURGERS

3 cups broiled mahi mahi
3 T onion, finely chopped
3 T dill pickle, finely chopped
1 T parsley, minced
salt and pepper to taste
¼ cup mayonnaise
1 egg, beaten

Shred mahi mahi with fingers. Combine fish, onion, pickle, parsley, salt and pepper, mayonnaise, and egg. Mix well. Form into patties. Fry or broil.

MAHI MAHI
BURGER #2

3 cups broiled Mahi Mahi
1/4 cup almonds or macadamias, chopped
1/4 cup pineapple, crushed
1/4 cup mayonnaise
1/2 t curry powder
1 egg, beaten

Shred Mahi Mahi with fingers. Combine fish, nuts, pineapple, mayonnaise, curry, and egg. Mix well. Form into patties. Fry or broil.

FISH FILLETS WITH SHRIMP

8 small fillets of sole
½ lb fresh mushrooms, chopped
½ lb fresh shrimp, deveined
4 T butter
4 T flour
1 cup milk
1 t salt
1 T lemon juice
chopped parsley

Cut 4 squares of aluminum foil. Arrange 2 fillets in each piece of foil. Sauté mushrooms in butter. Place mushrooms and shrimp on top of each fish package.

Combine butter, flour, milk, and salt. Heat, stirring constantly. When thickened, add lemon juice. Pour over fish, mushrooms, and shrimp. Sprinkle with parsley. Gather edges of foil together over fish, making a double fold for a tight seal. Fold ends. Place on a baking pan. Bake at 425° for 40 minutes. When ready to serve, slit top and open. Serves 4.

SHRIMP WITH PINEAPPLE

1 lb fresh shrimp, shelled and deveined
1 egg, slightly beaten
½ cup cracker meal
½ cup flour
1 t salt
2 cups oil
1 T sugar
½ t salt
1 T vinegar
½ cup water
½ red chili pepper
2 cups pineapple, cubed
1 T cornstarch
1 T water
Chinese parsley

Cut shrimp in half lengthwise. Toss shrimp in egg. Let stand 20 minutes. Combine cracker meal, flour, and salt. Roll shrimp in mixture. Deep fry in oil until golden brown. Combine sugar, salt, vinegar, water, and chili pepper. Add pineapple. Cook 10 minutes. Mix cornstarch and water. Add, and bring to a boil. Spread on serving platter. Put shrimps on top. Garnish with Chinese parsley. Serves 6.

CHINESE LOBSTER

2 lobster tails, cubed

1 onion, sliced

2 T oil

½ lb bean sprouts

¾ cup mushrooms, cooked

3 T soy sauce

1½ T cornstarch

Cook lobster and onion in oil in a covered pan or wok, until no longer crisp. Add bean sprouts and mushrooms. Blend soy sauce and cornstarch. Add. Toss all ingredients together over very hot fire for 1 to 2 minutes. Serve over steamed rice. Serves 4.

BARBECUED FISH

2 to 3 lbs fresh halibut, mahi mahi, swordfish
Marinade of your choice, preferably one with sherry and ginger

Arrange fish in baking dish. Pour marinade over fish. Marinate 1 hour. Remove and place on oiled grill over hot coals. Brush frequently with marinade. Barbecue 10 to 15 minutes. Turn carefully with spatula. Barbecue 10 or 15 minutes. Remove from grill with spatula. Brush with marinade. Serves 6.

FILLET OF SOLE

4 sole fillets
salt and pepper
1 T lemon juice
4 T butter
1 T lemon juice
¼ cup heavy cream
1 avocado, peeled, and sliced lengthwise
¼ cup macadamia nuts, coarsely chopped
lemon wedges

Sprinkle fish with salt and pepper and lemon juice. Let stand 10 minutes. Coat fish in flour. Brown fish in butter in frying pan. Place fish on hot platter. Sprinkle with lemon juice. Add cream to frying pan. Bring to boil, scraping browned particles loose. Spoon over fish. Garnish with avocado, nuts, and lemon. Serves 4.

BROILED FISH STEAKS

2 lbs swordfish, bass, salmon, or haddock, cut into steaks
3 T soy sauce
3 T sherry
2 T lemon juice
1 T oil
½ T fresh ginger, finely chopped
½ T sugar
3 green onions, sliced fine
lemon slices
green onions, cut in 1" pieces

Place fish in shallow dish. Combine soy sauce, sherry, lemon juice, oil, ginger, sugar, and onions. Pour over fish. Marinate, turning fish several times, 1 hour at room temperature. Place lemon and onions on fish. Grill fish over hot coals 4" from heat, 10 to 15 minutes on each side. Brush several times with marinade. Fish can be broiled, using a greased broiler pan. Serve with fried rice. Makes 6 servings.

STEAMED MULLET

2 lbs fresh mullet
2 t salt
1 t sugar
1 T oil
2 T soy sauce
4 T chung choy, finely chopped
4 T fresh ginger, chopped
4 T green onions, chopped
Chinese parsley
lemon wedges
2 T oil

Sprinkle salt over fish. Allow to stand for a few minutes in a shallow dish. Combine sugar, oil, and soy sauce. Pour over fish. Top with chung choy, ginger, and onions. Steam for 15 minutes. Heat oil. Pour over fish. Garnish with Chinese parsley and lemon wedges. Serves 6.

FISH BAKED IN TI LEAVES

2½ lbs white fish
1½ T rock salt
Ti leaves or aluminum foil

Prepare ti leaves by removing mid rib from back of leaves. Rub fish with salt. Wrap fish in several ti leaves. Tie the ends together with string or fibrous parts of ti leaves. Bake in shallow pan at 350° for 1 to 1½ hours. Makes 6 servings.

Variation: Add bacon slices or onion slices or coconut milk to fish before wrapping in ti leaves or foil.

TUNA AND PINEAPPLE CASSEROLE

1 can tuna, drained
1 cup pineapple chunks
1/3 cup blanced almonds, slivered
salt & pepper to taste
1 pkg frozen peas, thawed
1 can cream of celery soup, undiluted
1/4 cup pineapple chunks

Combine tuna, pineapple, almonds, salt and pepper, peas and soup. Mix gently. Pour into 1 quart casserole. Top with pineapple. Bake at 325° for 20 minutes.

QUICK AND EASY CHINESE-STYLE CASSEROLE

1 pkg frozen peas, thawed

2 cups celery, diced

1 onion, diced

1 green pepper, sliced

1 cup mushrooms, fresh or canned, sliced

1 can cream of mushroom soup

1 t salt

1 t garlic powder

1 pkg chow mein noodles

Place peas in botton of casserole. Add celery, onion, green pepper and mushrooms in layers. Heat soup. Add salt and garlic powder. Pour slowly over vegetables. Cover with noodles. Bake at 375° for 30 minuts. Serves 4.

COCONUT SHELL BAKE

6 coconuts

½ cup coconut water

12 fresh mushrooms, sliced

1 bell pepper, chopped

1 onion, chopped

1 clove garlic, minced

1 pkg. petite pois, frozen

2 T cornstarch

1 large chicken, cooked

3 carrots, sliced

1 t basil

½ t nutmeg

1 t parsley

sherry

½ pt half-and-half

salt to taste

Punch eyes out of coconuts. Drain coconut water and save. Saw off tops of coconuts 1″ below eye holes.

Combine cornstarch and coconut water. Place in top of double boiler. Cook until thickened to consistency of gravy. Add more coconut water if too thick. Add chicken, mushrooms, pepper, onion, garlic, peas, carrots, basil, nutmeg, parsley, sherry, half-and-half, and salt.

Fill coconut shells to top.

Make a paste of flour and water. Seal tops of coconut shells to bottoms with paste. Place in roasting pan in ½″

water. Cook at 300° for 3 hours. Remove 2 hours before serving. They will continue to cook in the sealed shell. When ready to serve, remove tops with chisel and hammer.

Serve coconut shell in a rice bowl, or make twisted rings of paper or napkins to hold coconuts upright on plates.

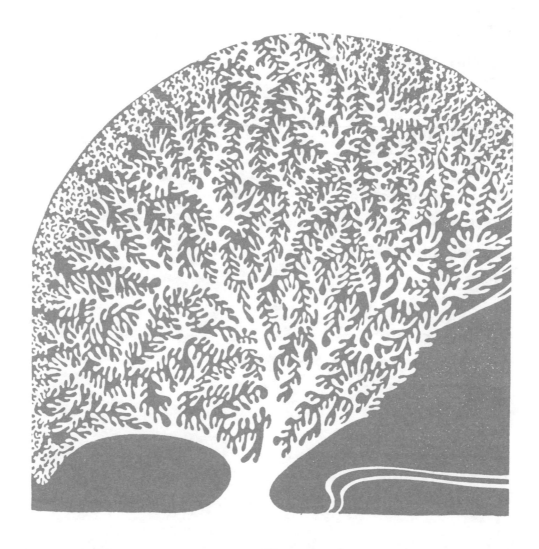

MARINADES

UNCOOKED MARINADES

#1

1 T sherry

2 T soy sauce

2 T sugar

1-1/2 t salt

1/2 t cinnamon

#2

1/4 cup soy sauce

1 T honey

1/4 cup chili sauce

#3

1/4 cup soy sauce

2 T brown sugar

2 jiggers sherry

#4

1/4 cup soy sauce

1/4 cup sherry

1/3 cup honey

1/2 t powdered ginger

#5

2 cups soy sauce

1 cup pineapple juice

1/2 cup sherry

1-1/2 T brown sugar

1 clove garlic, crushed

1/2 t ginger

#6

2 cups oil

2 cups red wine

1 cup soy sauce

2 cloves garlic, minced

1 onion, sliced

2 T lemon juice

SOY SAUCE AND GINGER MARINADE

1½ cups soy sauce

1 cup water

1 cup sherry

¼ cup sugar

2″ piece of ginger root, sliced

1 T green chiles, chopped

1 clove garlic, minced

1 onion, sliced

Combine soy sauce, water, sherry, sugar, ginger root, chiles, garlic, and onion in a saucepan. Bring to boiling. Reduce heat. Simmer 15 minutes. Cool. Leave steaks, chicken or pork in this marinade 3 to 4 hours at room temperature. Turn occasionally.

BASIC SOY SAUCE MARINADE

2 cloves garlic, mashed
4 T sugar
1 star anise*
1 T sherry
1½ cups soy sauce
1 cup water

Put garlic, sugar, anise, sherry, soy sauce, and water into a saucepan. Bring to a boil. Simmer uncovered for 5 minutes

*available at Asian grocery stores.

KOREAN MARINADE

3 T sesame seeds, toasted
3 T oil
1/4 cup soy sauce
1/3 cup onion, finely chopped
1/4 cup green onion, finely chopped
1 clove garlic, crushed
1/4 t pepper
1 slice ginger root, slivered
2 t sugar

Combine sesame seeds, oil, soy sauce, onion, green onion, garlic, pepper, ginger root and sugar.

TERIYAKI MARINADE #1

½ cup dry sherry

¾ cup soy sauce

3 T bottled steak sauce

2 T sugar

2 cloves garlic, crushed

Combine sherry, soy sauce, steak sauce, sugar, and garlic.

TERIYAKI MARINADE #2

½ cup soy sauce

2 T sugar

1 clove garlic, crushed

1 small piece ginger root, crushed

Combine soy, sugar, garlic and ginger root.

SAUCES

CHINESE MUSTARD SAUCE #1

1/3 cup dry mustard
1 T honey
2 t vinegar
1/4 cup water, cold
pinch of tumeric

Mix mustard, honey, vinegar, and water until well blended. Add tumeric for added yellow color.

CHINESE MUSTARD SAUCE #2

6 T boiling water
2 T dry mustard
1/2 t salt
2 t oil
pinch of tumeric (optional)

Stir boiling water and dry mustard. Mix well. Add salt and oil. Mix well. Add tumeric for added yellow color.

SWEET AND SOUR
SAUCE #1

1 cup hot water

1/2 t Worcestershire sauce

1/3 cup pineapple juice

1/4 cup mustard

1 t soy sauce

1/4 cup cold water

1 T vinegar

2 T cornstarch

Combine hot water, Worcestershire sauce, juice, vinegar, soy, and mustard. Heat. Mix cornstarch with water. Add to sauce. Cook 10 minutes.

SWEET AND SOUR
SAUCE #2

3/4 cup pineapple juice, unsweetened

1/4 cup cider vinegar

1 T soy sauce

2 T sugar

1/4 cup sweet red pepper, shredded

1/2 cup beef broth

2 T fresh or crystallized ginger, finely chopped

2 T cornstarch

1/3 cup water

Combine juice, vinegar, soy sauce, sugar, pepper, broth, and ginger in saucepan. Bring to boiling. Mix cornstarch and water. Add to boiling sauce, stirring constantly. Continue cooking and stirring for about 1 minute, or until sauce is thickened and clear. Makes 2 cups.

TANGY BARBECUE GLAZE

2 T oil
1 onion, finely chopped
2 cloves garlic, finely chopped
1 cup bottled chili sauce
1/2 cup lemon juice
1/3 cup molasses
3 T mustard
1 T Worcestershire sauce
1/4 cup dark rum

Saute onion and garlic in oil 5 minutes until soft. Stir in chili sauce, lemon juice, molasses, mustard and Worcestershire sauce. Bring to boiling.Cover. Simmer 20 minutes. Remove from heat. Stir in rum.

ORANGE-PINEAPPLE GLAZE

1 can frozen pineapple juice concentrate, undiluted
½ cup orange marmalade
2 T Worcestershire sauce

Combine juice, marmalade, and Worcestershire sauce in saucepan. Cook, stirring constantly, until mixture is thoroughly heated.

POLYNESIAN GLAZE

1 jar apricot preserves
1 cup pineapple, crushed
½ cup catsup
4 T vinegar
2 T Worcestershire sauce
1 t ground ginger
1 t dry mustard

Combine preserves, pineapple, catsup, vinegar, Worcestershire sauce, ginger, and mustard in small saucepan. Heat to boiling, stirring constantly. Lower heat. Simmer 1 minute.

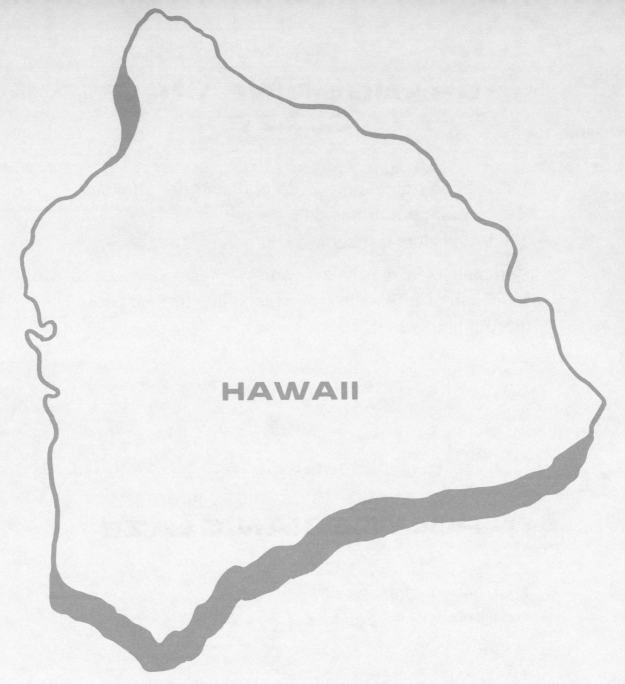

HAWAII

THE BIG ISLAND
OR THE ORCHID ISLAND

Flower—Lehua   Birthplace of King Kamehameha

Color—Red   Akaka Falls   City of Refuge

Kilauea Volcano   Kona Coast   Black Sand Beach

SIDE DISHES

SAIMIN

6 cups chicken or beef stock
1 T soy sauce
1 piece ginger root
1 lb fresh egg noodles, parboiled
½ t sesame oil
salt and pepper to taste
3 T green onions, chopped
½ lb. red pork or Chinese barbecued pork

Heat stock, ginger root, and soy sauce to boiling. Add noodles. Bring to almost boiling. Remove from heat. Mix in oil, salt and pepper. When ready to serve add onions and pork.

AVOCADO SOUP

1 avocado
1 onion, sliced
1 quart half-and-half
3 T sherry
dash of tabasco

Mix avocado and onion in blender until smooth. Add half-and-half gradually. Blend in sherry and tabasco. Chill well before serving. Serves 6.

PORTUGUESE BEAN SOUP

2 ham hocks

2 Portuguese sausages, sliced

3 qts water

2 cans kidney beans or 1 pkg. red kidney beans, soaked
    overnight

1 onion, cut up

1 clove garlic, mashed

2 potatoes, cut up

2 carrots, cubed

4 tomatoes, diced

several sprigs of parsley

salt and pepper to taste

Put water in a Dutch oven or large saucepan. Add hocks and sausage. Cook 3 hours over low heat. Add beans, onion, garlic, potatoes, carrots, parsley, and tomatoes. Cook 1 hour. Serves 8.

GAZPACHO SOUP
WITH AVOCADO

6 tomatoes, peeled and cut up

2 cups beef stock

3 T lemon juice

2 T oil

½ cup onion, minced

2 avocados, cut up

1 pint sour cream

Blend tomatoes and broth in blender. Add lemon juice, oil, and onion. Blend well. Stir in diced avocado. Chill several hours. When ready to serve, add a dollop of sour cream to each serving. Serves 6.

TOFU SOUP

1½ cups fish, cubed

5½ cups hot water

1½ t salt

3½ cups watercress, finely chopped

1 T soy sauce

tofu, cut in 1″ cubes

Add fish to water and salt. Steam 15 minutes. Add watercress, soy sauce, and tofu. Bring to boiling. Serve immediately. Makes 6 servings.

BAKED BREADFRUIT

1 ripe breadfruit
1 T lemon or lime juice
½ t cinnamon
2 T butter

Twist and pull stem to remove core of breadfruit. Cut in half lengthwise. Place in baking pan. Sprinkle with lemon and cinnamon. Dot with butter. Bake at 350° for 1 hour. Baste occasionally. Serves 4.

CURRIED RICE WITH ALMONDS

3 cups cooked rice

3 T butter, melted

¼ t curry powder

¼ cup parsley, minced

1 t salt

¼ toasted almonds, finely chopped

Blend butter and curry powder. Add to rice. Mix in parsley, salt, and almonds. Bake at 350° for 25 minutes. Serves 6.

FRIED RICE

4 cups rice, cooked

2 t salt

2 eggs

1 t sherry

1 T green onions, minced

4 T oil

Combine rice, salt, eggs, sherry, and onions in a large bowl. Mix thoroughly, using a wooden spoon. Place oil in a wok or skillet and heat at high temperature. Add rice mixture. Stir constantly for 8 minutes, or until grains separate. Serves 4.

CHICKEN LONG RICE

1 large chicken
1 cup chicken stock
1 cup water or more as needed
1 bundle long rice
2 onions, chopped
1 green onion, cut in strips
1 pkg Chinese peas
1/4 lb fresh mushrooms, sliced
2 T butter
salt and pepper to taste
Chinese 5 spice (optional)

Cut chicken into pieces. Brown. Add chicken broth and water to cover. Cook until tender. Soak long rice in bowl of cool water while chicken is cooking. Remove chicken from bones. Strain broth.

Sauté onions, green onion, and mushrooms in butter until soft. Add to broth. Add chicken. Simmer 10 minutes. Add long rice and peas, salt and pepper and 5 spice. Cook 15 minutes. Long rice absorbs liquid. If it becomes too dry, add boiling water. Serve in large soup bowls. Serves 6.

HAWAIIAN RICE WITH YOGURT

1 onion, minced

1 garlic clove crushed

3 T oil

1 cup water

2 cups pineapple juice

1 cup rice, uncooked

½ t ginger, ground

1 cup pineapple chunks

½ cup macadamia nuts or peanuts

1 cup yogurt

Sauté onion and garlic in oil until soft. Add water and juice. Bring to boil. Add rice and ginger. Cook over low heat, covered, 40 minutes. If liquid is not absorbed, cook longer. Mix pineapple, nuts, and yogurt. Heat. Serves 6.

CHINESE EGGS

6 hard cooked eggs
marinade of your choice

Put eggs in bowl. Cover with marinade. Marinate 24 hours. Cut into quarters.

LOMI SALMON

¼ lb smoked salmon
½ onion, thinly sliced
2 green onions, chopped (include green part of stalk for
     about 2″ above white)
2 tomatoes, cubed
6 ice cubes

Shred salmon with fingers. Place in bowl. Add onions and tomatoes. Press *(lomi)* or mash slightly with fingers. Put ice cubes on top. Refrigerate. Serve in small side dishes with some of liquid. Serves 6.

For the aloha touch, serve in a large seashell, or individual seashells.

ABALONE WITH CUCUMBERS

¼ lb abalone
1 t ginger, finely chopped
½ cup white vinegar
2 T sugar
¼ t Ajinomoto
½ t salt
3 cups cucumbers, thinly sliced
1½ T soy sauce

Cut abalone into small, thin slices. Combine ginger, vinegar, sugar, and Ajinomoto. Add fish. Marinate 30 minutes. Add cucumbers. Let stand 15 minutes. Press excess liquid from cucumbers. Pour on soy sauce. Chill. Makes 6 servings.

POLYNESIAN GREEN BEANS

1 pineapple
¼ cup onions, chopped
2 T butter
¼ cup sugar
¼ cup vinegar
1 T soy sauce
1 t dry mustard
1 T cornstarch
1 can water chestnuts, drained and sliced
1 lb green beans, cooked and sliced diagonally

Cut pineapple in half lengthwise. Retain leaves, cutting through them. Remove fruit. Be careful not to pierce shell. Dice ½ cup pineapple. Measure ¼ cup juice. (Reserve remaining pineapple for use in another recipe.) Sauté onion in butter until soft. Stir in sugar, vinegar, soy sauce, and mustard. Combine cornstarch with pineapple juice until smooth. Stir into onion mixture. Bring to boil, stirring constantly. Add pineapple, water chestnuts, and beans. Heat thoroughly. Heat pineapple halves at 350° for 10 minutes.

For the aloha touch, serve in pineapple shells.

BAKED BANANAS

12 bananas
lemon juice
1½ cups grated fresh coconut

HOT LEMON SAUCE
½ cup sugar
1 T cornstarch
¼ t salt
1 cup hot water
1 t grated lemon rind
3 T lemon juice
2 T butter

Cut each banana in half. Roll in lemon juice, then in coconut. Place in baking pan. Bake at 400° for 15 minutes.

Meanwhile, combine sugar, cornstarch, salt, and hot water. Cook 15 minutes, stirring constantly. Remove from heat. Stir in lemon rind, juice, and butter. Pour over bananas. Makes 6 servings.

BANANA SWEET POTATO CASSEROLE

4 large sweet potatoes
salt and pepper
4 large bananas, sliced
¼ cup butter
¼ cup brown sugar*
½ cup pineapple *or* orange juice *or* sherry

Parboil sweet potatoes. Peel. Cut in ¼" slices. Salt and pepper to taste. Layer in a casserole as follows: sweet potatoes, butter, bananas, brown sugar. Top with a banana layer. Over this pour, juice or sherry, depending upon the flavor you want. Bake ½ hour at 350° until brown. Serves 6.

For a spicy flavor, add ¼ t ground cloves and ½ t cinnamon to the brown sugar.

BANANAS BAKED IN ORANGE JUICE

2 bananas,* peeled
1 orange, peeled and cut in chunks
2 T orange juice
2 T lemon juice
1/3 cup sugar
dash of cinnamon
dash of nutmeg

Arrange bananas in a shallow baking dish. Add orange and lemon juices, sugar, cinnamon, and nutmeg. Bake 25 to 30 minutes, or until bananas are golden and tender. Serve hot or cold.

Use slightly underripe bananas—green-tipped or yellow, not flecked with brown.

BANANAS BAKED WITH SKINS

6 bananas, unpeeled

Wash bananas. Place unpeeled bananas in a shallow baking pan. Bake at 350° for 15 to 20 minutes. Remove from oven. Split lengthwise. Serve hot. Eat out of the skin, as a potato, with a fork.

Variation: Bananas may be roasted on outdoor barbecue grill over medium coals.

CURRIED BANANAS

½ cup orange juice

½ cup dry white wine

½ cup light brown sugar, firmly packed

3 T butter, melted

2 T lemon juice

¾ t curry powder

6 bananas, green-tipped

Combine orange juice, wine, sugar, butter, lemon juice, and curry powder in a saucepan. Simmer until thick and syrupy. Peel bananas and cut in half lengthwise. Arrange in a buttered baking dish. Pour on syrup. Bake uncovered at 350° for 20 minutes. Baste often. Makes 6 servings.

BANANA FRITTERS

1 cup flour

1 T sugar

1 egg, slightly beaten

½ t salt

½ cup water

1 t baking powder

6 bananas

½ t ginger or almond extract

butter

Sift together flour, sugar, and salt. Mix egg and water. Add to flour mixture. Mix thoroughly. Add extract. Cut bananas lengthwise, then in half. Dip bananas in batter. Fry in butter until golden brown.

SEA LETTUCE WITH RICE CAKES

sea lettuce, gathered on beach
1 cup rice, boiled
soy sauce

Sea lettuce is green in color, and grows at the half-tide mark. Summer is the best time to gather it.

Wrap boiled rice in sea lettuce. Serve with soy sauce.

DRIED SEA LETTUCE

sea lettuce, gathered on the beach

Place lettuce in collander or strainer. Blanch by pouring boiling water over lettuce. Spread aluminum foil on a cookie sheet. Bake in oven at 250° until crunchy. During the summer, it can be sun dried. Use to season salads, or like potato chips for munching.

PICKLED JAPANESE SEAWEED

Gather seaweed in the spring.

4 cups seaweed
4 cups boiling water
1 cup cider vinegar
1 cup brown sugar
½ t salt
¼ cup cucumber, finely sliced
¼ cup carrot, grated
2 T saki (optional)

Wash seaweed thoroughly. Put in strainer or collander. Blanch with boiling water. Drain. Place vinegar, brown sugar, and salt in a saucepan. Simmer 2 minutes. Remove from heat. Cool. Add cucumber, carrot, saki, and seaweed. Mix well.

TARO CAKES

3 cups cooked taro, mashed
1½ t salt
8 slices bacon

Fry bacon until crisp. Save drippings. Chop bacon. Blend taro, salt, and bacon. Shape into cakes. Fry until browned in bacon drippings. Makes 6 servings.

SWEET POTATO KABOBS

4 sweet potatoes or yams
6 bananas, green-tipped
3 limes
½ cup butter. melted
¼ cup pineapple juice, unsweetened
2 T brown sugar

Parboil sweet potatoes 25 minutes or just until tender. Drain. Cool and peel. Peel bananas. Cut potatoes and bananas into 1″ to 1½″ pieces. Cut each lime into 4 wedges, then cut each wedge in half crosswise. Thread potatoes, bananas, and limes onto skewers. Combine butter, concentrate, and sugar. Heat until blended. Brush part over bananas and sweet potatoes. Place skewers on grill, 4″ to 6″ from heat. Grill 10 minutes, or until heated through. Turn and baste often. Makes 12 servings.

HAWAIIAN CORN

2 cups corn kernels, cooked
½ t salt
1 T butter
½ cup coconut milk
½ cup fresh coconut, grated

Combine corn, salt, butter, coconut milk, and coconut. Heat thoroughly. Do not boil. Makes 6 servings.

BAKED PAPAYA

1 papaya, half ripe
salt
½ t ground ginger
1 t lemon juice
2 T butter

Cut papaya in half lengthwise. Remove seeds. Slice into serving pieces. Place in greased baking pan. Sprinkle with salt, ginger, and lemon juice. Dot with butter. Bake at 375° for 20 minutes, or until tender. Baste occasionally. Serves 4.

COCONUT FRITTERS

1/2 cup flour
1/2 t salt
2 t sugar
1/4 t baking powder
1 cup coconut, grated
1/3 cup evaporated milk
1 T butter, melted
2 eggs, separated
oil for deep frying

Sift flour, salt, sugar, and baking powder together. Add coconut, milk, and butter. Whisk egg yolks slightly. Add. Blend thoroughly. Fold in slightly beaten egg whites. Drop by tablespoon into hot oil (350°). Deep fry until golden. Makes 14 fritters.

OAHU

THE GATHERING PLACE

Flower—Ilima

Color—Yellow

Honolulu—State Capital

Diamond Head and Punch Bowl   Nuuanu Pali

Polynesian Cultural Center   Waikiki

Makaha   Bishop Museum

SALADS
SALAD DRESSINGS

CHICKEN SALAD WITH PINEAPPLE

1 chicken, cooked and cut in bite size pieces.

2 t mustard

6 T white vinegar, preferably wine

½ cup oil

1 t soy sauce

2 T honey

2 cloves garlic, crushed

2 cups pineapple, cubed

2 T raisins

4 T macadamia nuts, chopped

In a large bowl combine mustard, vinegar, oil, soy sauce, honey, and garlic. Mix well. Add chicken, pineapple, and raisins. Allow to stand 15 minutes. Turn once or twice so marinade will cover ingredients. When ready to serve, stir in macadamia nuts.
Put into papaya boats or coconut shells or leaves of lettuce. Serves 6.

CHICKEN CURRY SALAD

3 cups cooked white rice

3 whole chicken breasts, cooked and cubed

2 pkg frozen peas

1½ cups celery, chopped

½ cup white wine vinegar

½ cup mayonnaise

1 t curry powder

salt and pepper

¼ cup raisins

¼ cup slivered almonds

Combine rice, chicken, peas, celery, ginger, and mayonnaise. Add salt, pepper, and curry powder. Toss. Sprinkle with raisins and almonds. Refrigerate 1 to 2 days.

FRUIT SALAD
WITH SOUR CREAM

1 can mandarin oranges, drained
2 bananas, sliced
1 cup pineapple, crushed
1 cup coconut, flaked
1 papaya, diced
1 cup sour cream or yogurt

Combine oranges, bananas, pineapple, coconut, papaya. and sour cream. Cover. Refrigerate 6 hours or longer. Serve on bed of lettuce or in *hollowed out pineapple shell.* Garnish with coconut. Makes 6 servings.

CABBAGE AND
PINEAPPLE SALAD

2 cups cabbage, shredded
1½ cups cucumbers
1 small onion, thinly sliced
1½ cups pineapple, diced
5 T French dressing
lettuce
grated coconut

Combine cabbage, cucumbers, onion, and pineapple. Add French dressing. Toss gently. Serve on lettuce. Top with coconut. Makes 6 servings.

ISLAND SALAD

4 cups pineapple, cubed
2 cups tomatoes, cubed
1 T onion, grated
3 T lemon juice
3 T catsup
½ cup cream
salt and pepper

Place pineapple and tomatoes in a bowl. Sprinkle with onion. Combine lemon juice, catsup, cream, and salt and pepper. Blend well. Pour over pineapple and tomatoes. Chill. Makes 6 servings.

AVOCADO AND MELON SALAD

1 cup watermelon balls
1 cup cantaloupe balls
1 cup pineapple chunks
1/4 cup macadamia nuts
1/2 cup celery, sliced
2 avocados, halved *not* peeled
5 T French dressing

Combine melon balls, pineapple, nuts, and celery. Toss lightly with French dressing. *Fill avocadoes with fruit mixture.* Makes 4 servings.

LETTUCE, AVOCADO, WATERCRESS & KIWI SALAD

2 large heads Boston lettuce
2 large avocados, sliced
2 T lemon juice
2 large bunches watercress
4 kiwi, pared & sliced
2 cups celery, cut diagonally
¼ cup sesame seeds, toasted
Pineapple-Lemon-Mint dressing

Line large salad bowl with large outer leaves of lettuce. Tear remaining leaves into bowl. Sprinkle avodado slices into lemon juice. Remove large stems from watercress. Arrange avocados, watercress, kiwis, and celery on lettuce. Sprinkle with sesame seeds. when ready to serve, shake Pineapple-Lemon-Mint dressing. Pour over salad. Toss gently.

PICKLED CUCUMBERS

1 cucumber, thinly sliced
3 T salt
3 T sugar
3 T vinegar

Sprinkle cucumber with salt. Let stand ½ hour. Rinse off salt. Drain. Add sugar and vinegar. Chill thoroughly. Serves 4.

ORANGE AND ONION SALAD

Assorted lettuce, preferably romaine, butter and red
2 oranges
1 onion
lemon and oil dressing
mint sprigs

Wash and dry lettuce. Tear into bite size pieces. Place in bowl. Chill. Slice onion into very thin rings. Peel and slice oranges into very thin rings. When ready to serve, add oranges and onions to lettuce. Toss. Pour dressing over. Garnish with mint sprigs. Makes 4 servings.

PAPAYA AND NUT SALAD

1 papaya
½ cup salted peanuts, finely chopped
2 cups lettuce, coarsely cut
French dressing
lettuce

Chill papaya. When thoroughly chilled, remove seeds, and cut into small cubes. Blend with peanuts and lettuce. Toss lightly with French dressing. Serve on lettuce leaves. Makes 4 servings.

For the aloha touch, serve in papaya boats.

FRUIT SALAD WITH MARSHMALLOW DRESSING

1/2 watermelon

assorted sliced peaches, strawberries, papaya cubes, cantaloupe and watermelon balls, diced pineapple, sliced kiwi, tangerine sections, sliced bananas, grapes.

1 pt. fruit sherbet (preferably pineapple)

DRESSING*

1 cup sugar

2/3 cup light corn syrup

1/3 cup hot water

2 egg whites

dash of salt

1/4 t vanilla

1/4 cup mayonnaise

1 T orange rind, grated

Halve a watermelon, with the cup running lengthwise. Fill with assorted fruits. Chill thoroughly

Combine sugar, corn syrup, and hot water. Heat slowly, until sugar dissolves. Boil until syrupy. Beat egg whites and salt until stiff. Gradually beat in syrup*. Add vanilla. Cool. Fold in mayonaise and orange rind.

*If you are in a hurry, substitute a jar of marshmallow topping and then add the vanilla, mayonnaise and orange rind.

JELLO HAUPIA KANTEN

FIRST LAYER

3 oz lime jello

1 cup water

1/3 cup sugar

Combine and boil until sugar is dissolved.

1/2 cup water

1 envelope unflavored gelatin

Combine and add to jello.

Pour into pan and chill until set. This will take about 1 hour.

SECOND LAYER

2 pkgs instant Haupia mix

1 3/4 cup water

Cook until thick. Allow to cool. Gradually spoon over first layer.

THIRD LAYER

3 oz strawberry jello

1 cup water

1/3 cup sugar

Combine and boil until sugar is dissolved.

1/2 cup water

1 pkg gelatin

Combine and add to jello.

Allow to cool until lukewarm. Spoon over Haupia (second layer).

BANANA AND BACON SALAD

4 bananas
2 oranges, sectioned
salad greens
⅓ cup salad oil
¼ cup white wine vinegar
2 T bacon bits
1 T chives, minced

Peel and slice bananas lengthwise. Arrange with orange sections on salad greens. Combine salad oil, vinegar, bacon bits and chives. Mix until well blended. Pour over fruit.
Makes 4 servings.

TURKEY SALAD

3 cups cooked turkey, diced
1 can water chestnuts
½ cup celery, chopped
¾ cup macadamia nuts
2 T vinegar
2 T crystallized ginger
¾ cup mayonnaise
1 t curry powder
1 T soy sauce
1½ cups pineapple, diced

Combine turkey, water chestnuts, celery and nuts. Add vinegar. Mix well. Add ginger. Combine mayonnaise, curry powder, and add pineapple and soy sauce. Add to turkey mixture. Mix thoroughly. Chill several hours. Serve on lettuce or in *hollowed out pineapple shell.* Makes 8 servings.

SPINACH SALAD DRESSING

2 to 3 bunches fresh spinach
2 t onion, grated
1 t salt
½ t pepper, freshly ground
2 T prepared mustard
2 T wine vinegar
8 T oil
¼ t lemon juice
fresh mushrooms

Combine onion, salt, pepper, mustard, vinegar, oil, and lemon juice in a large screw top jar. Cover. Shake thoroughly. Add mushrooms. Refrigerate until ready to use. Toss with spinach.

PINEAPPLE-LEMON-MINT DRESSING

¾ cup oil

¼ cup pineapple juice, unsweetened

2 T lemon juice

1 t lemon peel

1 t dried mint, crumbled

¾ t salt

½ t dry mustard

Combine oil, pineapple and lemon juices, lemon peel, mint, salt, and mustard in a large screw top jar. Cover. Shake thoroughly. Refrigerate until ready to use.

POPPY SEED DRESSING

1/3 cup honey

1 t salt

2 T vinegar

1 T mustard

1/4 cup oil

1 T onion, finely chopped

3 t poppy seeds

Combine honey, salt, vinegar, mustard, oil, onion, and poppy seeds in blender. Blend until smooth.

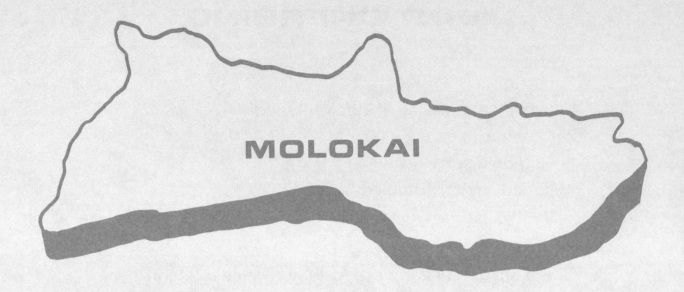

THE FRIENDLY ISLAND

Flower—Kukui or candlenut

Color—Green

Kalaupapa   Moaule and Hipuapua Falls

Halawa Valley Palaau Park

Wailau Valley

BREADS

PORTUGUESE PAN DULCE
now known as
HAWAIIAN SWEET BREAD

8 cups flour

6 eggs, slightly beaten

½ lb. butter

2 cups sugar

2 yeast cakes or envelopes

2 cups milk, warm

1 cup cooked mashed potatoes

½ t salt

1 egg white beaten

Dissolve yeast in ½ cup warm milk. Sift flour, sugar, and salt together. Add butter and potatoes. Add yeast and milk to eggs. Mix. Pour into flour/potato mixture. Mix. Knead until dough does not stick to hands. Allow to rise until double in bulk. Put into greased round cake pans. Let rise again. Brush tops with egg whites. Bake at 375° for 45 minutes, or until done. Watch carefully, it browns easily.

"PUKA PUKA PANCAKES"

Give waffles or "puka puka pancakes" the aloha touch with the following variations.

— add 1 cup shredded coconut to batter
— add 2/3 cup drained crushed pineapple to batter
— add grated rind of 1 orange and 2 t orange juice to batter
— add chopped walnuts, peanuts, pecans, or macadamia nuts to orange batter. Garnish with nuts when serving.
— add ½ cup macadamia nuts to batter. Garnish with macadamias when serving.

BANANA BREAD

2 cups cups sugar
1 cup shortening
6 bananas, mashed
4 eggs well-beaten
2½ cups cake flour
2 t baking soda

Combine sugar, shortening, bananas, and eggs.Mix well. Sift together flour, salt, and baking soda. Blend with banana mixture. *Do not overmix.* Pour into 2 greased and floured loaf pans. Bake at 350° for 45 to 50 minutes. Remove from oven. Leave in pan for 5 minutes. Remove. Cool on rack.

BANANA MUFFINS

2 cups flour
1/4 cup sugar
1-1/2 t baking powder
1/2 t baking soda
1/2 t salt
1 egg, beaten
3/4 cup milk
1/2 cup banana, mashed
1/3 cup macadamia nuts, chopped
1/4 cup shortening, melted
2 t lemon juice

Sift together flour, sugar, baking powder, baking soda and salt. combine egg, milk, banana, shortening, and lemon juice. Pour into flour mixture. Stir only until flour is moistened. Put liners in muffin tins. Fill each muffin cup 3/4 full. Bake at 425° for 20 minutes. Serve warm. Makes 24 muffins.

PINEAPPLE NUT BREAD

2 cups flour

1/2 cup sugar

1 t baking powder

1/2 t salt

1 cup raisins or dates chopped

1/2 cup macadamia nuts, chopped

1 egg beaten

1 t vanilla

2 T shortening, melted

1 cup pineapple, crushed and not drained

1 t baking soda

Sift together flour, sugar, baking powder, and salt. Add raisins and nuts. Combine egg vanilla, and shortening. Add to flour mixture. Dissolve soda in pineapple. Stir until blended. Pour into greased loaf pan. Bake at 350° for 1 hour or until done. Remove from oven. Leave in pan 5 minutes. Remove. Cool on rack.

MIA'S PINEAPPLE BRAN MUFFINS

1 cup bran

1 cup buttermilk

1 cup flour

1 t cinnamon

1 t baking powder

1/2 t baking soda

1/2 t salt

1/3 cup butter

1/2 cup brown sugar

1 large egg

1/4 cup molasses

1/4 cup pineapple

1/3 cup chopped dates or raisins

GLAZE

1/2 cup honey

2 T corn syrup

1 T butter

Combine bran and buttermilk. Mix together flour, cinnamon, baking powder, baking soda, and salt. Add, all at once, to bran mix. Stir just until blended. Cream butter, sugar, egg, and molasses thoroughly. Blend into bran mixture. Stir in pineapple and dates. Put liners in muffin tin. Fill each muffin cup 3/4 full. Bake at 400° for 20 to 25 minutes. Cool slightly. Remove liners.

Melt honey, corn syrup and butter in saucepan. Simmer 5 minutes. Place muffins, one at a time, in glaze coating thoroughly. Place on a cookie sheet until glaze is set. Serve warm. Makes 12 muffins.

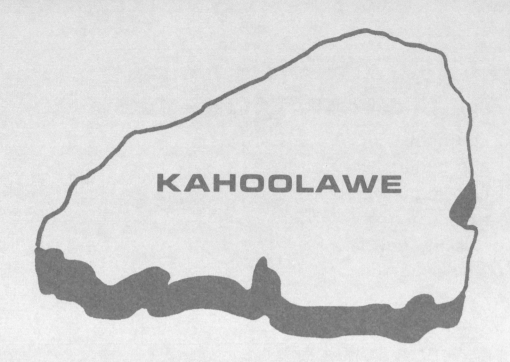

KAHOOLAWE

THE FORBIDDEN ISLAND

Flower—Hinahina Vine

Uninhabited.

Used by Navy as a bombing target.

DESSERTS

PIÑA COLADA MOUSSE

2 t gelatin, unflavored

2 T rum

½ cup coconut pineapple juice
  or ½ cup pineapple juice and
    ½ cup coconut milk

½ t vanilla

2 egg yolks, beaten

3 T sugar

½ cup whipping cream

mint sprig

In upper portion of a double boiler, combine gelatin and rum. Let stand to soften. Place double boiler oven low heat. Stir until completely dissolved. Stir in juice, vanilla, egg yolks and sugar. Cook until slightly thickened. Remove from heat. Set upper portion of double boiler aside to cool. Whip cream. Fold gently into mixture, a third at a time. Chill thoroghly Garnish with mint. Serves 2.

HAUPIA

2 T cornstarch or arrowroot
3 T sugar
⅛ t salt
2 cups coconut milk

Make smooth paste of cornstarch, sugar, salt and ½ cup coconut milk. Scald remaining milk over low heat, stirring rapidly. Add mixture to scalded milk. Cook over low heat until clear. and coats spoon. Pour into a shallow pan. Refrigerate until firm. Makes 6 servings.

PAPAYA WHIP

⅛ t salt
2 egg whites
½ cup sugar
1½ cups papaya pulp*
1 t lemon rind, grated
juice of 1 lemon
grated coconut (optional)

Beat egg whites and salt until stiff. Gradually add sugar, beating until mixture forms peaks. Fold in papaya. Add rind and juice. Chill. Makes 6 servings.

*for the aloha touch, leave some papaya in the shell. Spoon whip into shell when ready to serve.

MANGO BETTY

4 cups bread cubes, toasted
1 ½ cups cooked prunes, pitted and chopped.
1 ½ cups mangoes, sliced
2 ½ cups prune juice
¾ cup sugar
½ t salt
½ t cinnamon
2 T butter
2 T lemon juice
1 T lemon rind grated

Place ½ toasted bread cubes in greased baking dish. Put down a layer of prunes, then a layer of mangoes with remaining bread cubes. Combine prune juice, sugar, salt, cinnamom and butter. Boil 3 minutes. Stir in lemon juice and rind. Pour over contents in baking dish. Bake 350° for 45 minutes. Serves 8.

COCONUT MACAROONS

½ cup sweetened condensed milk
2 cups coconut, grated
1 t vanilla

Combine milk, coconut,and vanilla. Drop by spoonfuls 1″ apart on greased cookie sheet. Bake at 350° for 10 minutes, or until delicately browned. Cool on rack. Makes 2 dozen cookies.

BANANA DROP COOKIES

1 1/4 cups sugar

2/3 cup shortening

1 t vanilla

2 eggs

1 cup *ripe* bananas, mashed

2 1/4 cups flour

2 t baking powder

1/4 t baking soda

1/2 t salt

1 cup macadamia nuts, chopped

1/4 cup sugar

1/2 t cinnamon

Cream together sugar, shortening, and vanilla until light and fluffy. Add eggs. Beat well. Stir in mashed bananas. Sift flour with baking powder and soda and salt. Add. Mix well. Stir in the nuts. Chill 30 minutes. Drop by teasponfuls 2″ apart on greased cookie sheet. Mix sugar and cinnamon. Sprinkle over unbaked cookies. Bake at 400° for 8 to 10 minutes, or until lightly browned. Makes 5 dozen cookies.

DATE NUT CHEWS

2 eggs
1/2 t salt
1/2 t almond extract
1/2 cup sugar
1/2 cup corn syrup
1 cup dates, finely chopped
1 cup macadamia nuts, chopped
3/4 cup flour
1/3 cup powered sugar

Place eggs in large mixing bowl. Add salt and almond extract. Beat until light and frothy. Gradually beat in sugar and corn syrup. Add dates and nuts. Mix well. Fold in flour. Pour into two 8″ cake pans. Bake at 375° for 25 minutes. Remove from oven. Cut into 1½″ bars immediately. Shape at once into small balls. Roll into powered sugar. Makes 3 dozen cookies.

MACADAMIA NUT CLUSTERS

¼ lb semi-sweet chocolate
½ cup sweetened condensed milk.
1 cup whole macadamia nuts, unsalted

Melt chocolate over low heat. Remove from heat. Add milk and nuts, stirring constantly. When thickened, drop by teaspoonfuls on greased cookie sheet. Chill thoroughly. Makes 2 dozen.

TROPICAL COOKIES

3 cups flour

1 T baking powder

1 t salt

1 cup butter

2/3 cup sugar

2/3 cup light brown sugar, firmly packed

1 t vanilla

1 egg

3/4 cup macadamia nuts, finely chopped

Sift together flour, baking powder, and salt. Cream butter and sugars until fluffy. Blend in vanilla and egg. Gradually blend in flour mixture. Stir in nuts. Divide dough in half. Shape each half into a 1½" roll. Wrap in plastic or wax paper. Chill 4 hours, or until firm. Preheat oven to 350°. Slice rolls into ¼" slices. Place slices on ungreased cookie sheet. Bake at 350° for 10 or 12 minutes. Cool on wire rack. Makes 7 dozen cookies.

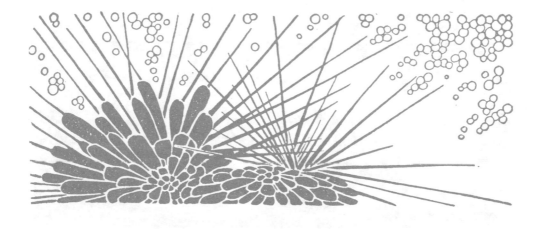

GINGER BARS

1 cup dark brown sugar, firmly packed

1 egg

2 T butter

¼ cup molasses

1 t vanilla

1 cup flour

½ t salt

½ t baking soda

½ t cinnamon

½ t ginger, ground

¼ t cloves, ground

¼ cup milk

1 cup nuts, coarsely chopped

Mix together sugar, egg, butter, molasses, and vanilla. Sift flour with soda, salt, cinnamon, ginger and cloves. Add alternately with milk. Mix well. Stir in nuts. Pour into greased 9″ square pan. Bake at 350° for 35 to 40 minutes. Cool in pan. Makes 2 dozen bars.

BANANA CHIFFON CAKE

2 1/4 cups cake flour, sifted

1 cup sugar

3 t baking powder

1 t cinnamon

1/2 t salt

1/2 cup oil

5 egg yolks

2 T lemon juice

3 bananas mashed

8 egg whites

1/2 t cream tartar

1/4 cup sugar

Sift flour, sugar, baking powder, cinnamon, and salt into a medium bowl. Make a well in the center. Add in order oil, egg yolks, lemon juice, and bananas. Beat with spoon until smooth.

Beat egg whites and cream of tartar until foamy. Gradually beat in sugar, until meringue forms soft peaks.Fold egg yolks mixture gently into meringue, until no streaks of white remain. Spoon into an ungreased 10" tube pan. Bake at 325° for 1 hour and 10 minutes, or until top springs back when lightly pressed with finger tip. Invert pan, placing tube over a funnel or large bottle. Let cake cool completely. Loosen around the cake with spatula.

PAPAYA CHIFFON PIE

3 eggs, separated

¼ cup sugar

2 T lemon juice

1 t grated lemon rind

3 T hot water

½ T unflavored gelatin

2 T cold water

1¾ papaya pulp

¼ cup sugar

9" pie shell baked

In a saucepan beat yolks until thick. Add sugar, lemon juice, lemon rind, and water. Cook over low heat until thickened. Soak gelatin in cold water. Stir into hot mixture until dissolved. Add papaya. Cool. Beat egg whites until foamy. Slowly beat in sugar. until meringue forms peaks. Fold in papaya mixture. Pour into pie shell. Chill until firm.

MANGO CHIFFON PIE

5 cups mango slices, half-ripe

½ cup sugar

3 eggs, separated

3 T water

¼ cup sugar

2 t gelatin, unflavored

3 T cold water

1 T lemon juice

¼ cup sugar

9″ pastry shell, baked

Combine mango slices and sugar. Let stand 20 minutes. Cook over low heat until tender. Cool. Put through sieve or puree in blender. In a sauce pan beat egg yolk slightly. Add water and sugar. Cook over low heat until thickened. Soak gelatin in water. Stir into hot mixture until dissolved. Add lemon juice and mango sauce. Blend in. Refrigerate until slightly set. Beat egg whites until foamy. Gradually beat in sugar until stiff. Fold into mango mixture. Pour into pastry shell. Chill until firm.

MIA'S MAUI MUD PIE

CRUST

21 Oreo cookies

1/2 stick butter, melted

Crush cookies. Mix thoroughly with butter. Press into a 9" pie pan. Make sure bottom and sides are evenly coated and pressed very firmly. Place in freezer for at least overnight. *It must be frozen firm.*

FILLING

2 pts coffee ice cream

Soften slightly. Transfer to pie shell. Spread into the crust, mounding it a bit higher in the middle. Return to freezer.

GLAZE

1 square unsweetened chocolate

2 squares semi sweet chocolate

1 1/2 T water

2 T corn syrup

1 1/2 T butter

Combine water, corn syrup and butter. Heat until bubbly. Add chocolate. Stir until melted. Remove from heat. Cool to room temperature. Pour glaze *carefully* over frozen ice cream until ice cream is covered with a very thin layer. Return to freezer. Chill at least 2 hours. When ready to serve, top with whipped cream flavored with rum or Kahlua.

FRESH PINEAPPLE PIE

3 cups fresh pineapple, finely chopped
3 T cornstarch
½ cup sugar
¼ t salt
Pastry for a 2 crust 9" pie

Cook pineapple until tender, and consistency of canned crushed pineapple. Drain. Mix cornstarch, sugar, and salt. Add to pineapple. Cook until thick, stirring constanly. Cool. Pour into pie shell. Cover with top crust. Bake at 425° for 25 minutes.

MANGO PIE

¾ cup sugar
1 t cinnamon
2 T lemon juice
4 half ripe mangoes, sliced
1 T butter
Pastry for 2 crust 9" pie

Combine sugar, cinnamon, and lemon juice. Mix with mango slices. Put in pastry shell. Dot with butter. Cover with top crust. Seal edges. Cut vents to allow steam to escape. Bake at 425° for 45 minutes.

MAI TAI PIE

1 envelope gelatin, unflavored

1/4 cup sugar

4 eggs, separated

1 can pineapple juice, unsweetened

1/4 cup fresh lime juice

1/3 cup light rum

2 T orange-flavored liqueur or cointreau

1/4 cup sugar

1/2 cup cream, whipped

Mix gelatin and sugar in small pan. Beat in egg yolks until well blended. Gradually blend in pineapple juice. Cook stirring constantly, until gelatin disolves and mixture is slightly thickened. Do not boil. Remove from heat. Stir in lime juice, rum and liqueur. Pour into large bowl. Chill, stirring often, until mixture starts to thicken. While gelatin mixture chills, beat egg whites until foamy. Slowly beat in sugar until meringue forms soft peaks. Fold meringue and whipped cream into gelatin mixture. Spoon into cooled coconut shell. Chill at least 3 hours.

COCONUT CRUST

1 cup flaked coconut

6 T butter, melted

Blend coconut and butter. Press onto bottom and sides of a 9″ pie plate. Bake at 300° for 25 minutes or until golden brown. Cool on a wire rack.

COCONUT PIE

1/4 cup butter
1/2 cup powered sugar
4 cups coconut, grated
2 egg whites
1/2 cup powered sugar
Pastry for 2 crust 9" pie

Cream butter and sugar. Add coconut. Blend thoroughly . Beat egg whites until foamy. Slowly beat in sugar until meringue forms soft peaks. Fold meringue into coconut mixture. Place in pie shell. Cover with pastry. Bake at 425° for 35 minutes.

MACADAMIA NUT PIE

½ cup butter softened
¾ cup light brown sugar, firmly packed
¾ cup light corn syrup
¼ cup honey
4 eggs beaten
1 t vanilla

1 can macadamia nuts, coarsely chopped

Beat butter and sugar until creamy. Beat in corn syrup and honey. Next, beat in eggs and vanilla. Stir in nuts. Pour into pie shell. Bake at 425° 10 minutes on bottom rack of oven. Lower oven to 325°. Continue baking for 25 minutes, or until golden brown. Cool before serving.

CHOCOLATE MERINGUE PIE

2 egg whites

⅛ t salt

⅛ t cream tartar

½ cup of sugar

½ cup macadamia nuts, finely chopped

½ t vanilla

1 pkg (¼ lb) sweet chocolate

3 T water

1 t vanilla

1 cup whipping cream

Combine egg whites, salt, and cream of tartar in mixing bowl. Beat until foamy. Add sugar 2 T at a time, beating after each addition until mixture stands in very stiff peaks. Fold in nuts and vanilla. Spoon into lightly greased 8" pie pan. Make a nestlike shell, building sides up ½" above edge of pan. Bake in slow oven a 300° for 50 to 55 minutes. Cool to room temperature.

Place chocolate and water in saucepan over low heat. Stir until chocolate is melted. Cool until thickened. Add vanilla. Whip cream. Fold chocolate mixture into cream. Pile into meringue shell. Chill at least 2 hours before serving. *This pie may be prepared the day before and refrigerated.*

KONA COFFEE
ICE CREAM PIE

3 pints vanilla ice cream

1 ½ cups heavy cream

½ cup macadamia nuts, coarsely chopped

2 T coffee liqueur

2 T instant coffee

4 egg whites

¼ t cream of tartar

½ cup sugar

9" pastry shell, baked

Soften 1 pint ice cream in a medium size bowl. Beat ½ of the heavy cream in a small bowl until stiff. Fold into softened ice cream along with nuts and liqueur. If very soft, place in freezer until mixtures holds its shape. Soften remaining 2 pints ice cream in large bowl. Stir instant coffee into remaining heavy cream. Beat until stiff. Fold into remaining softened ice cream. Spread 2/3 of coffee mixture in rolled pastry shell. Make a depression in center. Spoon macadamia mixture into center. Mound remaining coffee mixture on top. Freeze overnight or until firm. Beat egg whites and cream of tartar until foamy. Beat in sugar until meringue forms soft peaks. Cover ice cream filling with meringue and maraschino cherries in proportions desired. Chill.

PINEAPPLE BAKED ALASKA

1 angel food cake
1 can pineapple, sliced
1 pint vanilla ice cream
3 egg whites
3 T sugar
1 t cream of tartar
¼ t salt

Cut circles of cake the same size as pineapple slices. Drain pineapple. Place on serving dish or foil covered baking board. Combine egg whites, salt, and cream of tartar in mixing bowl. Beat until foamy. Add sugar, a little at a time, beating until mixture stands in stiff peaks. Top pineapple with scoops of very hard vanilla ice cream. Cover completely with meringue. Put under broiler until meringue browns. Watch constantly. Serve immeddiately.

MACADAMIA ICE CREAM

3 egg yolks
¾ cup sugar
2½ cups milk, hot
1 t vanilla
2 cups heavy cream, whipped
¾ cup rum
¾ cups macadamia nuts, chopped

Beat egg yolks with sugar in upper portion of double boiler until light. Gradually stir in hot milk. Cook until thick. Mixture should coat spoon. Add vanilla. Cool. Fold in cream. Put in freezer compartment of refrigerator. When almost frozen, beat in rum and nuts. Freeze until firm. If using ice cream freezer, put cooled custard in to freezer and crank until almost frozen. When almost frozen, add rum and nuts. Crank until firm.

COCONUT ICE CREAM

3 cups coconut milk
1½ cups coconut water
1 cup sugar
¼ t salt
½ t vanilla

Combine coconut milk, water, sugar, salt, and vanilla. Stir until sugar is dissolved. Freeze until firm. Beat 3 times during freezing process. Serves 6

FROZEN PAPAYA CREAM

2 papayas
¼ cup lemon juice
½ cup sugar
1 cup light cream

Cut papayas in half lengthwise. Scoop out seeds. Scoop out pulp. Puree papaya with lemon juice and sugar in blender until smooth. Stir in cream. Pour mixture into a 9″ x 9″ x 2″ pan. Place in freezer 1 hour. Remove. Stir with spoon until smooth. Return to freezer another hour or until softly frozen. Spoon into chilled medium size bowl. Beat with electric mixer until smooth, 1 to 2 minutes. Spoon into plastic container or bowl. Cover. Serve softly frozen or freeze until firm, (6 hours or overnight). Serves 6.

PAPAYA SHERBERT

1 papaya
juice of 2 oranges
juice of 1 lemon
1 cup sugar
2 cups cream

Puree papaya in blender. Add orange and lemon juices and sugar. Blend well. Blend in cream. Pour into freezer tray. Freeze overnight. Stir once during freezing. Makes 6 servings.

Variation: Substitute 1/2 cup pineapple juice or crushed pineapple for orange and lemon juices.

MANGO SHERBERT

2 large mangoes
1/2 cup sugar
1/2 cup water
1/4 cup lemon juice
1/2 cup sugar
1/3 cup water
1/4 t salt
2 egg whites

Peel and slice mangoes. Whip in a blender until smooth. Add sugar, water, and lemon juice. Blend until sugar is dissolved. Pour into a freezer tray. Freeze to mush. Boil sugar and water until it forms a thick syrup. Add salt to egg whites. Beat until stiff. Pour syrup slowly over egg whites, beating constantly. Beat until mixture is cool. Fold into fruit mixture. Freeze. Stir once during freezing. Makes 6 servings.

AVOCADO ICE CREAM

An original recipe by Ruth Drown Gally

2½ cups milk

2 level T cornstarch

½ cup of sugar

2 eggs, well beaten

1 envelope unflavored gelatin

¼ cup water

4 drops almond extract

¼ cup dry sherry

3 T lemon juice

2 avocados. or enough to make 1 cup mashed avocados

Soften gelatin in water. Heat milk, cornstarch, and sugar in upper section of double boiler. Stirring constantly. Add eggs. Beat with electric beater. Add gelatin and almond extract. Continue beating 2 minutes. Put bowl in refrigerator to cool. When cooled and set beat several minutes. Add avocados, lemon juice, and sherry. Beat three minutes. Add cream. Beat until thick, but not stiff. Place in freezing compartment of refrigerator. Leave for an hour or so. Remove, then stir well and beat several more minutes. Put in container and return to freezer. Makes 3 pints.

Instructions for Ice Cream Freezer. After custard is cool, add remaining ingredients and crank. Remove dasher. Pack freezer. Best if allowed to "ripen" several hours.

Serve in cantaloupe halves

PINEAPPLE COCONUT SUNDAE

1 cup pineapple, crushed
½ cup syrup from pineapple
½ cup pineapple
1 qt. vanilla ice cream
¼ cup coconut shredded
macadamia nuts, chopped

Combine pineapple, syrup, and sugar. Cook over low heat about 20 minutes. Cool. Stir in coconut. Pour over ice cream. Garnish with nuts. Makes 6 servings.

BANANAS WITH HONEY

8 bananas
juice of one lemon
2 T butter
1 cup honey
1 ¼ cups coconut, cream
1 cup coconut grated

Peel bananas. Cut into 1 ½" pieces. Place in greased baking pan. Sprinkle with lemon juice. Dot with butter. Cover with honey. Bake a 400° for 20 minutes. Top with coconut cream. Garnish with coconut. Serve hot. Makes 6 servings.

PINEAPPLE CHEESE CAKE

CRUST

2 cups graham cracker crumbs

1 cube butter, melted

1/2 cup powdered sugar

Combine ingredients until well blended. Press into bottom of springform pan. Chill for 30 minutes.

3 4 oz packages cream cheese, softened

2 eggs

1/2 cup sugar

2 cup crushed pineapple, drained

1/2 t cinnamon

1 pint sour cream

3 T sugar

1 t vanilla

Combine cream cheese, eggs, sugar, crushed pineapple and cinnamon. Beat until smooth. Pour into prepared crust. Bake at 375⁰ for 20 minutes. Cool for 1 hour. Mix sour cream, sugar and vanilla. Spread over cheesecake. Bake at 375⁰ for 5 minutes. Chill several hours.

MANDARIN ORANGES IN PAPAYA HALVES

papayas
2 cans mandarin oranges, drained.
mint sprigs

Cut papaya in half lengthwise. Remove seeds. Sprinkle with lemon juice. Fill with mandarin orange sections. Garnish with mint. Chill. Serves 4.

ORANGE SLICES IN CURACAO

6 oranges, peeled and sliced
¼ cup curacao
½ cup grated coconut
Marinate oranges for a least 12 hours. Sprinkle with coconut.

Makes 6 servings.

PINEAPPLE IN GINGERED YOGURT

2 cups yogurt, plain
4 large pieces crystallized ginger, cut up
1/2 cup pineapple, crushed

Drain pineapple. Mix yogurt, ginger, and pineapple together. Put in freezer tray. Leave in freezer until barely set. Serves 4.

Variation: Use Piña Colada yogurt

DATE NUT TORTE

1 cup sugar
1/3 cup flour
1/8 t salt
1 T baking powder
2 eggs beaten
1 cup dates, cut up
1 cup macadamia nuts, chopped

Mix sugar, flour, salt, baking powder in a bowl. Add eggs. Mix well. Blend in dates and nuts. Spread in a buttered 8" by 8" pan. Bake at 325° for 35 to 45 minutes.

FRESH FRUIT PARFAIT

bananas, sliced
strawberries, sliced
peaches, sliced
watermelon balls
cantaloupe balls
pineapple chunks
papaya sliced
1/4 cup of orange juice
3 T sugar
1 T lemon juice
1/3 cup cointreau

Fill jar or container with bananas, strawberries, peaches, watermelon, cantaloupe, pineapple and papaya. Combine orange juice, sugar, lemon juice, and cointreau. Mix well. Pour over fruit. Cover. Refrigerate several hours. Stir occasionally.

QUICK COCONUT CANDY

1/2 lb marshmallows
4 cups coconut, grated

Melt marshmallows over low heat. Add coconut. Stir until blended. Drop by spoonfuls on foil or waxed paper. Store in refrigerator. Makes five dozen candies.

ISLAND DELIGHT

pineapple chunks
dates, chopped
bananas, sliced
coconut shredded
maraschino cherries, halved

Combine pineapple, dates, bananas, coconut, and maraschino cherries in proportions desired. Chill.

For the aloha touch, serve in hollowed-out pineapple shell.

BRANDY FROST

1 quart vanilla or coffee ice cream, softened
½ cup brandy
½ cup creme de cacao
chocolate square

Combine ice cream, brandy and creme de cacao in blender. Blend until smooth. Pour into chilled glasses. Garnish with grated or curled chocolate. Serve with straws. Serves 8.

NIIHAU

ISLAND

OF

MYSTERY

Flower—sea shell (pupu)

Color—white

Privately owned by Robinson Family since 1863

Halalii Lake

BEVERAGES

COFFEE FLOAT
WITH RUM

4 T instant coffee

10 T brown sugar

4 cups milk

2 T dark rum

1 pint coffee ice cream

Blend coffee, sugar, milk and rum in blender for 15 seconds. Pour into tall glasses. Top with ice cream. Serves 4.

HAWAIIAN COFFEE

2 cups coconut milk

2 T sugar

2 cups strong Kona coffee, hot

Bring coconut milk *just* to boiling point, stirring constantly. *Overheating will cause curdling.* Add sugar to coffee. Combine milk and coffee. Makes 6 servings.

To serve chilled, do not heat milk. Use cold coffee. Whirl in blender for 10 seconds.

COFFEE SMOOTHIE

2 cups strong Kona coffee, cold

2 bananas (optional)

1 pint coffee ice cream, softened

Blend coffee, bananas, and ice cream throughly in blender for 30 seconds, or until smooth. Serves 4.

HAWAIIAN COFFEE

An original recipe by Ruth Drown Gally

1 gallon strong Kona coffee, hot

10 drops almond extract

½ cup creme de cacoa

1 cup sugar

½ cup cocoa

1 t salt

3 trays coffee ice cubes made with Kona coffee

1 pint whipping cream

Simmer almond extract, creme de cacoa, sugar, cocoa, until well blended. Refrigerate. Whip cream until firm, but not stiff. Fold into coffee mixture. When ready to serve, put ice cubes in punch bowl. Pour in chilled coffee mixture. Makes 30 servings.

ICED COFFEE WITH SPICES

3 cups strong Kona coffee, hot
2 cinnamon sticks
4 cloves
4 whole allspice
2 t Kahlua
crushed ice or ice cubes

Pour coffee of cinnamon sticks, cloves, and allspice. Let stand 1 hour. Strain. Add Kahlua. Pour over ice in tall glasses. Serves 4.

HOT FRUIT TEA WITH RUM

4 cups tea, hot
1/2 cup sugar
1 cup orange juice
1/3 cup pineapple juice
1 cup light rum
lemon slices

Add sugar, orange and pineapple juices, and rum to tea. Garnish with lemon slice. Serve hot.

MENUS

BRUNCH

Silver Sword Fizzes

Fruit Salad with Marshmallow Dressing

or

Island Salad

Linguisa Omelette

Sliced Avocados and Sliced Tomatoes

Banana Muffins

Kona Coffee

BARBECUE BRUNCH

Champagne or Orange Juice

Fruit Salad in Pineapple Shells

Shrimp Kabobs

Pineapple Bran Muffins

Fried Rice

Rumakis

Date Nut Torte

LARGE BRUNCH

Champagne

Pineapple Bran Muffins

Grilled Grapefruit

Banana Fritters

Chutney Baked Ham

or

Sweet and Sour Pork Chops

Scrambled Eggs with Chives

Toasted Hawaiian Bread

Kona Coffee

SMALL LUNCHEON

Frozen Daiquiris
Crab Stuffed Mushrooms
Macadamia Cheeseballs
Pineapple Nut Bread with Cream Cheese
Turkey Salad
Date Nut Torte   Mango or Pineapple Sherbert
Orange Spiced Tea

LUNCH
FOR A GROUP

Aloha Fruit Punch or Champagne Sherbet Punch
Sesame Chicken Wings
Hawaiian Short Ribs
Chicken Curry Salad
Banana Bread
Jello Haupia Kanten
Pineapple Cheese Cake
Coffee Hawaiian

FISH DINNER

Rumaki
Pickled Cucumbers, Curried Nuts
Avocado Soup
Fillet of Sole
Chinese Snow Peas with Water Chestnuts
Fried Rice
Tossed Green Salad with lemon and oil dressing
Kona Coffee Ice Cream Pie

FISH BARBEQUE

Scorpion   Chi Chi   Beer
Teriyaki Kabobs
Chicken Wings in Soy Sauce
Vegetable Sticks with Curry dip
Barbecued Mahi Mahi or Swordfish
Barbecued Corn
Barbecued Bananas
Avocado and Grapefruit Salad
Chiffon Pie

COCONUT SHELL BAKE

Coconut Shell Bake
Tossed Green Salad
French Bread
Avocado Ice Cream   Coconut Cookies
or
Pineapple Alaska

HAWAIIAN CURRY
DINNER

Chilled White Wine
Curry
Steamed Rice
chopped peanuts, chopped preserved ginger
chopped green pepper, raisins, dried apricots,
grated hard cooked eggs, toasted coconut,
crisp bacon bits, chutney
Bananas Baked in Skins
Orange and Onion Salad
Tropical Fruit Parfait with Cointreau
Pineapple in Gingered Yogurt
Tea
Coconut Macaroons
Chinese Almond Cookies

SUMMER SUPPER

Gazpacho soup
Chicken Salad in Papaya Boats
Fried Rice
Kona Coffee Popsicles
Fresh Coconut Pie
Iced Herb Teas or Hot Fruit Tea with Rum

WINTER DINNER

Hawaiian Cocktail #1 or #2 or Gin Aloha
Portuguese Bean Soup
Spinach Salad
French Rolls
Mango Chiffon Pie
Hawaiian Coffee

DINNER FOR TWO

ALOHA MEANS I LOVE YOU

Hawaiian Sunrise
cheese and crackers, ginger almonds, pickled prawns
Gazpacho soup
Lanai Sirloin Steak
or
Fish Fillets with Shrimp
Baked Papaya or Bananas in Orange Juice
Piña Colada Mousse or Chocolate Meringue Pie
Kona Coffee with Whipped Cream

Everything on this menu, except the cocktail, may be prepared ahead of time.

LUAU

Mai Tais Daquiris   Beer

Curried Peanuts, Roasted Macadamia Nuts

Fish Shaped Crackers, Chutney Cream Cheese Spread

Celery Carrots Green Pepper Cauliflower

Avocado Dip

Shrimp in Pineapple Shells

Meat Balls and Chestnuts in Chafing Dish

Lomi Salmon

Baked Sweet Potatoes

Kalua Pig

Chicken Luau

Slices of fresh pineapple, papaya, mango, banana

arranged on platter around Kalua Pig

Pineapple Sherbet Coconut Cake

Haupia

Coffee with Kaluha Liqueur

LUAU

Chicken Long Rice
Lau Laus
Hawaiian Sweet Potatoes with Pineapple
Hawaiian Fruit Bowl
Portuguese Sweet Bread
Mango or Guava Sherbert
or

Mandarin Oranges and Pineapple Chunks
in Papaya Halves
Banana Bread
Coffee

THE ALOHA TOUCH

PINEAPPLES
halakahiki

The color of the outer pineapple is not an indication of ripeness. A yellow bare and green upper portion are considered best, but the color may vary from green to golden.

The pineapple must sound solid when snapped with forefinger and thumb. Thump the inner side of your wrist, then the pineapple. If the sounds are similar, the pineapple should be good.

Another test is to tug one of the "leaves", wriggling it slightly from side to side. If it comes out easily, the fruit should be ripe.

Invest in a serrated pineapple knife. It will make coring and cutting pineapple much easier.

Use fresh pineapple whenever possible, not only to eat, but for decor. A scooped out pineapple, sliced lengthwise with crown attached, makes a striking container for a salad, dessert, or main dish.

PINEAPPLE SMOKE
halakahi'ki uwa'hi

After you have finished using scooped out pineapple shells as containers for serving, use them to prepare this unique flavoring for your barbecues.

Wash shells thoroughly, scraping away as much of the remaining meat as possible. Shred the exterior of the shell on a grater. Avoid grating the meat. This shredding can be done easily in a food processor.

Spread out on a baking pan or cookie sheet. Bake in oven for at 150° for 1 hour, or dry in sun. Store in air tight container. When ready to use, mix one cup with just enough water to moisten (about ⅛ cup). Let stand for 20 minutes. Sprinkle on top of hot barbecue coals, as you would hickory chips.

COCONUTS
niu

CRACKING COCONUT

Husk and remove loose fibers from coconut shell. Poke openings through the eyes and drain off the liquid. This is coconut *water*. Crack the nut by tapping around the middle with a hammer, until it splits in half.

REMOVING THE MEAT

BAKING METHOD: Remove coconut water. Place coconut in a shallow pan. Bake in oven at 300° for 45 minutes. Remove from oven. Crack open with hammer, unless coconut has already done so while baking. Remove meat with knife.

TAPPING AND SPLITTING METHOD: Tap the coconut shell all over the outside with hammer. This will help the meat come out in larger pieces. Crack shell into large pieces with hammer. Loosen meat with knife.

GRATING COCONUT THE HAWAIIAN WAY

Place Hawaiian grater on a chair. Sit on wooden part of grater to hold grater in place. Cup a coconut half in both hands. Scrape the meat over the metal grater. Grated coconut will drop into pan placed below grater. A damp cloth wrapped around the outside of the shell helps prevent bits of fiber from falling into the pan.

HOW TO MAKE A HAWAIIAN GRATER

Select a piece of wood about 1¼" thick and 14" square. Cut to shape shown. Plane until smooth. For the grater use a strong metal strip about 7″ long and 1½″ wide, curved slightly upward at one end. The curved end should have a saw-toothed edge. Each tooth should be about ⅛″ deep. The grater is firmly fastened onto the wooden seat. Or investigate acquiring an Hawaiian grater on your next trip to Hawaii.

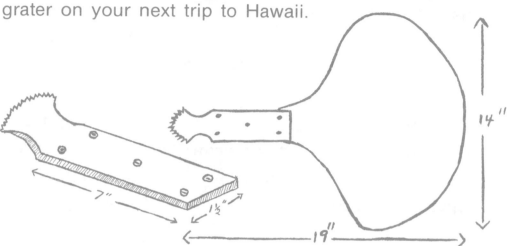

COCONUT WATER: Coconut water is the liquid drained from the coconut shell.

COCONUT MILK: Pour 2 cups boiling water over 4 cups grated coconut. Let stand 20 minutes. Strain through a poi cloth or a double thickness of cheese cloth. Press to remove liquid. Milk may be stored in the refrigerator for several hours before using, or frozen for 2 to 3 weeks.

If milk is to be heated, bring it just to the scalding point, stirring constantly, to avoid curdling.

COCONUT CREAM: Allow coconut milk to set for a few hours in the refrigerator. A thick, creamy substance will rise to the top. Skim this off. This substance is called coconut cream. It is good as a sauce or whipped after it has been chilled.

GINGER
awapuhi

Ginger root is readily available year around in the vegetable section of most markets. Hawaiian ginger is characterized by its plump size, hand like knobs and light brown color. However, since you will use it often, it is worth while to keep a supply in your freezer.

TO USE: *Do not defrost.* Grate off needed amount. Return unused frozen ginger root to freezer. Hold 1 T of grated ginger root in your palm. Add ¼ t cold water. Clench fist tightly, squeezing juice into container. Repeat as needed.

PAPAYAS
hei or papaia

When shopping, choose a papaya with some yellow color. Allow it to ripen until fully, or almost fully yellow. *Do not refrigerate.* When ripe, papaya should yield slightly to the touch.

Use papayas often. They are as rich in vitamin C as oranges, and are also rich in vitamin A and in potassium. Papaya adds a special flavor to muffins, breads, and drinks.

AVOCADOES
pea

Avocadoes ripen more quickly in a tightly closed brown paper bag.

Once avocadoes have been sliced, prevent darkening by brushing or sprinkling all cut surfaces with lemon juice. In addition, until ready to use, leave seed in if avocado is halved, or store removed seed with avocado slices.

SUGGESTIONS FOR THE ALOHA WAY

1. Buy soy sauce by the gallon or ½ gallon.

2. Keep a soy sauce bottle on the table.

3. Plant ginger, ti, and mint plants in pots or in your garden.

4. Explore using raw brown sugar when recipes call for brown sugar.

5. Keep a supply of frozen coconut milk in your freezer.

6. Keep a 15½oz. can of cream of coconut on hand for use with desserts and in tropical drinks.

7. Substitute spinach for taro leaves. Fresh is best, but frozen leaf spinach can be used.

8. Try using Hawaiian rock salt (pa'a kai)

9. Grow a ti plant. Start it with a ti root sold packaged in Hawaii. It is also available at many nurseries on the mainland.

10. The ti leaf imparts a delicious flavor to food when it is used as a wrapper. Fish and meat, wrapped in ti leaves and cooked in the oven, aquire a distinctive flavor. Banana leaves may be substituted for ti leaves.

11. Use *fresh* cocount and pineapple whenever possible.

12. Explore different flavors by substituting marinades.

13. Look for dried squid, dried abalone, Japanese fern bark, and octopus at Asian markets. They will add a particularly authentic touch. Try tofu, bok choy vegetables, Korean Kim Chi (pickled cabbage), crack seed, and passion fruit (lilikoi).

14. Macadamia nuts are very costly. Try substituting peanuts or almonds some of the time.

15. Invest in an Hibachi.

16. Grow Manoa lettuce (Dark Green Mignotte), Manoa Sugar Pea, Maui Onion (Texas Granex), and other plants from seed.

Seeds available from:

    Great Honolulu Seed and Plant Co.
    2431 University Avenue
    Honolulu, Hawaii 96882

    The Sandwich Islands Seed Co., Inc
    Postal Drawer 630
    Kailua, Oahu
    Hawaii 96734

ALOHA DECOR

Leis are always fun to give, and really help create an aloha mood. They can be made with many different things.

The most authentic leis are created with flowers, but if this isn't practical try wrapping unshelled peanuts, hard candy, gum, or money in squares of colored celophane or tissue paper. Twist the ends, and tie together with ribbons.

Flower-style leis can be made from crepe paper, and are an excellent way to keep children busy before it is time to eat. Cut crepe paper across package in one inch widths. Thread needle with doubled cotton thread. Thread through center of strips with small stitches. Push paper along thread, keeping it closely packed. When it is the desired length, twist paper to create spiral effect. Crepe paper or tissue paper can be cut in flower shapes and strung one by one, but this takes much longer.

To give a tropical feeling to an indoor party, use lots of greenery. Bamboo, cut five or six feet high, and massed in tall vases or containers in corners—sword ferns with birds of paradise or gladiolas—gardenias or camelias floating in large flat bowls—all create the atmosphere you want.

Tuck some ferns and hollyhock, carnations or other blossoms into bowls of fresh fruit. Place leaves and flowers around the base of your punch or salad bowls. This is the time to show off your house plants, particularly those that will cascade down book case shelves or mantels.

For a buffet, cover your table with a plain cloth, then use split bamboo or lauhala mats. For large picnic tables, tatami beach mats make interesting covers. Decorate by placing ti, canna or calla lily leaves or other large leaves down the center. Wallpaper, or wrapping paper with shell, fern, bamboo or tapa cloth motifs also make excellent table covers.

Tapa cloth can be simulated by drawing a repeat tapa design in heavily with black and brown crayons. When finished, crush and recrush paper until it is soft; then iron with a warm iron. It will look and feel very authentic.

Fruits and flowers can be placed on the leaves down the center of the table. Use wooden bowls if you have them. A pineapple makes a spectacular holder for toothpick appetizers. Hollow out a watermelon to use as a punch bowl, or to fill with fruit. Use avocado shells to hold dips.

To recreate a beach atmosphere, use driftwood, coral, fish nets and sea shells for table decorations. Add a small outrigger or canoe, or surfboard, a diving mask, ukelele, and fish-shaped crackers to your centerpiece.

Encourage everyone to wear aloha shirts, puka shell necklaces and mumus.

Play some Hawaiian records in the background, and you're back in the islands.

Ono KauKau.

INDEX

MUFFINS

Banana 129
Mia's Pineapple Bran 131

PUPUS

Beef Teriyaki 34
Butterflied Coconut Shrimp 32
Chicken Wings in Soy Sauce 38
Chutney Cream Cheese Spread 41
Coconut Chips 35
Cream Cheese Crisps 42
Curried Peanuts 39
Deviled Eggs 37
Macadamia Cheddar Cheese Balls 40
Meat Balls and Water Chestnuts 35
Mushrooms Stuffed with Crab 40
'Ono 'Ono Spareribs 30
Pineapple with Rum 41
Poison Creux 39
Pork Balls 36
Raw Fish 39
Roasted Macadamia Nuts 39
Fumaki 30
Seafood on a Skewer 33
Sesame Chicken Wings 37
Shrimp Kabobs 33
Teriyaki Ribs 31
Won Ton 31

SALADS

Avocado and Melon 115
Banana and Bacon 120
Cabbage and Pineapple 114
Chicken Curry 113
Chicken with Pineapple 112
Fruit with Marshmallow Dressing 118
Fruit with Sour Cream 114
Island 115
Jello Haupia Kanten 119
Lettuce, Avocado, Watercress and Kiwi 116
Orange and Onion 117
Papaya and Nut 117
Pickled Cucumbers 116
Turkey 121

SALAD DRESSINGS

Pineapple-Lemon-Mint 123
Poppy Seed 123
Spinach 122

SAUCES

Chinese Mustard #1 85
Chinese Mustard #2 85
Sweet and Sour #1 86
Sweet and Sour #2 87
Tangy Barbecue 88

SIDE DISHES

BANANAS
Baked 102
Baked in Orange Juice 104
Baked with Skins 104
Fritters 105
Casserole 103
Curried 105

FRUITS
Baked Bread Fruit 95
Coconut Fritters 109
Baked Papaya 109

FISH
Abalone with cucumbers 100
Lomi Salmon 99

RICE
Curried 96
Fried 96
with Yogurt 98

SEAWEED AND SEA LETTUCE
Dried 106
Pickled 107
with Rice Cakes 106

SOUPS
Avocado 92
Gazpacho 94
Portuguese Bean 93
Saimin 92
Tofu 94

VEGETABLES
Corn 108
Polynesian Green Beans 101
Sweet Potato Kebobs 108
Taro Cakes 107

MISCELLANEOUS

Chinese Eggs 99
Chicken Long Rice 97

WAFFLES

"Puka Puka Pancakes" 127

NOTES

NOTES

NOTES